Additional Praise for *The Development of Mexico's Tourism Industry: Pyramids by Day, Martinis by Night*

"Dina Berger's book is an important new study that explains how U.S. and Mexican elites transformed and marketed the image of revolutionary Mexico."

—Tom O'Brien, University of Houston

"How Mexico became one of the world's top tourist destinations is a fascinating and hitherto largely untold story. Thanks to Dina Berger's path breaking, deftly researched study, we can now trace the origins of Mexican tourism back to the dark days of the Mexican Revolution, when against all odds a dynamic group of revolutionaries, boosters, bankers, and entrepreneurs reinvented Mexico's tattered image, seduced the gringo tourist, and laid the foundations for a world-class industry. Berger's engaging account demonstrates that tourism was more than business: it was Mexico's ticket to modernity."

— Adrian A. Bantjes, University of Wyoming

"In an engaging and insightful example of cultural and political history, Dina Berger demonstrates how the Mexican leadership connected tourism with the construction of a new economy and broader polity because tourists demand creature comforts and their example would increase the material expectations of the general public. Under President Lazaro Cardenas the focus was widened to include the promotion of prehistoric sites and museums that not only promoted tourism but also created an increased sense of national cultural unity."

—John Mason Hart, Author of *Empire and Revolution: The Americans in Mexico Since the Civil War*

The Development of Mexico's Tourism Industry

Pyramids by Day, Martinis by Night

Dina Berger

palgrave
macmillan

First published in 2006 by
PALGRAVE MACMILLAN™
175 Fifth Avenue, New York, N.Y. 10010 and
Houndmills, Basingstoke, Hampshire, England RG21 6XS
Companies and representatives throughout the world.

PALGRAVE MACMILLAN is the global academic imprint of the Palgrave Macmillan division of St. Martin's Press, LLC and of Palgrave Macmillan Ltd. Macmillan® is a registered trademark in the United States, United Kingdom and other countries. Palgrave is a registered trademark in the European Union and other countries.

ISBN 1–4039–6635–4

Library of Congress Cataloging-in-Publication Data is available from the Library of Congress.

A catalogue record for this book is available from the British Library.

Design by Newgen Imaging Systems (P) Ltd., Chennai, India.

First edition: March 2006

10 9 8 7 6 5 4 3 2 1

Printed in the United States of America.

Transferred to digital printing in 2007.

To my parents, Carol and Paul,
and to my husband, Ingmar

A trip to Mexico without a visit to the native markets is as incomplete as a Martini cocktail with the olive left out.

Mexican Tourist Association, souvenir album, ca. 1939

Contents

LIBRARY

ILLUSTRATIONS

FIGURES

TABLE

Note on Currency

Currency Value Based on US$1.00

Year range	Average exchange rate from old Mexican Peso	Average relative value in 2003
1928–1931	MexS2.10	USS11.14
1932–1937	MexS3.52	USS13.49
1938–1945	MexS4.93	USS11.81

Note: For example, if the average price of a ticket for a tour through Mexico City in 1930 cost Mex$7.00, then it cost an American tourist about US$3.33. Today, that ticket would cost about US$36.76.

Source: Table based on currency value and exchange rate calculators published by Economic History Services (http://www.eh.net), an economic history website run by Miami University of Ohio and Wake Forest University. Authors of specific calculators are Saamuel H. Williamson, "What is the Relative Value?" Economic History Services, April 15, 2004 (http://www.eh.net/hmit/compare/) and Lawrence H. Officer, "Exchange rate between the United States dollar and forty other countries, 1913–1999." Economic History Services, EH.Net, 2002 (http://www.eh. net/hmit/exchangerates).

Acknowledgments

For the past five years, I have lived the study of tourism in Mexico. Like the development of the industry itself, I would not have been able to carry out this research and piece together this story if not for the vast network of colleagues, archivists, and friends across Mexico and the United States. What began as a story untold, turned into a history that touched on just about every aspect of Mexican culture, economics, history, and politics. I'd first like to thank Bill Beezley, my advisor for life, who more than anyone believed in this project and urged me to tell it, and who was kind enough to comment on earlier parts of this manuscript. I'd also like to thank my tourism *compadre*, Drew Wood, for helping forge the field of Mexican tourism history and for his many insightful comments on this manuscript. Andrea Boardman and Suzanne Kaufman also took the time to read and comment on earlier versions of this manuscript. Thanks also to the cohort of modern Mexican historians who, over the years, have helped me understand this subject matter better, especially Nikki Sanders, Victor Macías, Aaron Navarro, Julio Moreno, Eric Schantz, Ariel Rodríguez Kuri, Patrice Olsen, Rachel Kram, Anne Rubenstein, Susan Gauss, Monica Rankin, Jeff Pilcher, and Jim Garza.

I cannot thank enough the many archivists and friends in Mexico who went out of their way to help me track down the all-important document or the all-important contact. My heartfelt thanks also extends to the Pani family for opening their doors to me and for sharing their personal papers and stories. Jorge González, son of the well-known Mexican painter Jorge González Camarena, showed me warm hospitality when he met with me to discuss his father's work at *Galas de México*. Thanks to the many people who helped me untangle this story: Mónica López Velarde at Museo Soumaya, Lic. Eduardo Turrent y Díaz of the Banco de México, and Jaime Barceló of the Escuela Mexicana de Turismo. Thanks to the many archivists at the fantastic array of private and public libraries and archives around Mexico City, especially those at the Archivo General de la Nación and the Centro de Estudios de Historia de México CONDUMEX, where

I spent most of my time. Finally, I want to recognize my wonderful friends in Mexico who gave me a home away from home: Marisol, Mónica, Abe, and Luz María.

Funding for this project was made possible by awards from the David and Flora Hewlett Foundation, the College of Wooster, and the Clements Center-DeGolyer Library at Southern Methodist University. But the impetus to complete it was found in the support of my husband, cheerleader mom, and daughter, Amelie, whose recent arrival made its completion all the more meaningful.

Abbreviations for
Tourism-Related Organizations

AAMA   Asociación Automovilística Mexico-Americana (Mexican American Automobile Association)

AMA   Asociación Mexicana Automovilística (Mexican Automobile Association)

AMH   Asociación Mexicana de Hoteles (Mexican Hotel Association)

AMT   Asociación Mexicana de Turismo (Mexican Tourist Association)

CMPT   Comisión Mixta Pro-Turismo (Mixed Pro-Tourism Commission)

CNT   Comisión Nacional de Turismo (National Tourism Commission)

CPT   Comisión Pro-Turismo (Pro-Tourism Commission)

CTNT   Comité Nacional de Turismo (National Tourism Committee)

FFCCN   Ferrocarriles Nacionales de México (National Railways of Mexico)

MTA   Mexican Tourism Association

PEMEX   Petróleos Mexicanos (Mexican Petroleum Company)

INTRODUCTION

On October 2, 1938 at Chapultepec Castle, members of the U.S. and Texas Hotel Associations dined at the behest of President Lázaro Cárdenas. They were joined by dignitaries and their wives from Mexico's most important government institutions including the Interior and Foreign Affairs Ministries as well as representatives from that nation's most powerful financial institutions from mining to transportation. On behalf of the president, Ramón Beteta, sub-secretary of Foreign Affairs, greeted the guests with both optimism and amicability that belied emotions driving oil nationalization only months earlier. Beteta spoke about the mutual benefits of goodwill and friendship between people and nations inherent in tourism. He pointed out the emergence of a new, democratic Mexico that no longer eschewed poverty and inequality, noting that under its reform-minded president, tourists were encouraged to see Mexico, warts and all. Although not proud of its faults, Beteta stated, the president "feels that we are not to blame for the poverty prevailing in Mexico which is the result of centuries of ruthless exploitation."[1] In an effort to pull his nation out of this plight, he continued, President Cárdenas made holidaymaking easier by improving accommodations, building better highways, and making more accessible tourist attractions. According to Beteta, these changes in the development of Mexico's tourist industry were evidence that freedom was alive and well, particularly in contrast to other places in the world where "individual liberty is being trampled under foot."[2] In other words, Beteta made a connection between the development and promotion of the tourist industry, and travel itself, with democracy, civilization, and modernity, especially in contrast to the recent rise in totalitarianism, where people's movement was restricted.

Only months earlier on March 18, the same president who welcomed American hoteliers and who touted the benefits of tourism in Mexico sent shockwaves through the international community when he nationalized the petroleum industry. Amid unanswered demands for fair labor practices, Cárdenas asserted national sovereignty to the celebration of the Mexican people, many of whom voluntarily donated their personal belongings—jewelry and livestock—to help the government compensate American- and British-owned oil companies. In a patriotic move to gain control of Mexico's national industries from foreign imperialists, Cárdenas's oil, land, and railroad expropriations targeted U.S. corporate interests, with whom American hoteliers dining at Chapultepec Castle were akin. Returning to this gala event six months later, one might ask why the president would warmly receive the very hand that he worked to cut off. Did efforts to develop an industry like tourism not fly in the face of Cárdenas's nationalist cause and broader goals of the Mexican Revolution?

This study examines this question from the perspective of tourist developers and promoters like Beteta and Cárdenas. It shows how tourism appeared to be compatible with the goals of the revolution. The multiple groups that rose up against longtime president Porfirio Díaz in 1910 fought not for an atavistic Mexico but for a progressive, modern nation. Tourism, many argued, offered a means to become modern and to overcome serious financial problems left by fighting and a foreign debt made worse by the Great Depression. Moreover, tourist development and promotion under Mexican control would prove to be a viable, state-directed industry: an industry made by and for Mexicans. Motorists would drive on government-financed highways where they would buy gas at government-regulated Petróleos Mexicanos (Pemex) stations, rent rooms in government-licensed hotels built by Mexican companies, and eat at locally owned restaurants. Finally, tourism innately celebrated and evoked pride in things Mexican. Like the celebrated murals, folk art, films, and music, its tourist industry was inspired by and built on ideas of Mexican grandeur—vast beaches, curative waters, Mesoamerican pyramids, Indian villages and markets, colonial buildings, Porfirian monuments and boulevards, and modern constructs. These expressions of nationalism help explain why political elites who actually fought in a revolution to regain control of their nation from foreign interests became the most outspoken developers of an industry that catered primarily to these same foreigners.

To reconcile this contradiction, to win national support, and perhaps to justify their participation in the tourist industry, the victors of the revolution couched its development in patriotic language meant to evoke pride in the profitability of Mexico's natural assets. These revolutionary elites[3] argued that because the state founded, developed, and regulated its own tourist industry and promoted its own national attributes, Mexicans would act as agents in shaping their own path toward stability, prosperity, and modernity. Thus, tourism emerged as an industry that best embodied what historian Thomas O'Brien has described as the successful fusion of "nationalism and capitalism into a project of Mexican national development" by the 1940s.[4] Tourism demanded that Mexicans build highways, hotels, train stations, gas stations, boulevards, and airports; that they create skilled service jobs such as the trained, licensed and bilingual tour guide, hotel clerk, and wait staff; and that they construct first-class hotels, theatres, nightclubs, museums, and restaurants. Rather than a departure from long-established revolutionary goals linked to the countryside, tourism was an expression of revolutionary reconstruction rooted in capitalism, namely, economic development, urbanization, and personal advancement.

At the time, Beteta and others did not consider the underbelly of tourist development in a disadvantaged host nation that catered to privileged guests. While it undoubtedly modernized Mexico, tourism perpetuated ties of dependency as a service-oriented, demand-sided industry. While it strengthened the government, tourist development often led to dubious interests of a national and personal nature. And while it bolstered nationalism and internationalism, tourism prompted elites to devise an image of Mexico that fit within the parameters of tourists' desires. Tourism, as Dennison Nash and others have argued,[5] proved to be a kind of imperialism that contradicted and should have worked against revolutionary nationalism. Nevertheless, its development served a much larger purpose in the history of Mexico's national development. Not just a way to improve the national economy, tourism offered the state and the revolutionary elites a means to participate in modern capitalism, becoming what Nora Hamilton has called "revolutionary capitalists."[6] Tourism created a host of new jobs not only in the service industry but also in the construction of hotels, highways, and airports (today, it constitutes 10 percent of total national employment[7]). Even better, tourism did not require a factory for its production; rather, as an invisible industry and export it required relatively little investment from multiple sources. Money flowed in, and no product, save for a few souvenirs, had to be manufactured or sold. Finally, because tourism was exceptionally profitable (today, it generates an estimated US $73 billion USD in earnings[8]) it offered high returns and opportunities for personal advancement. With some investment, former presidents, ministers, and ambassadors became notable hoteliers, restaurateurs, and all-around tourist promoters.

* * *

The story of the development of Mexico's tourist industry unfolds during a most unlikely period—revolutionary state building—and involves a most unlikely cast of historical actors—the revolutionary elites, an array of government officials, business leaders, intellectuals, journalists, and artists, in cooperation with American corporate and government interests and well-connected friends of Mexico. In particular, the creation of a tourist industry emerged as the cornerstone to state-led modernization programs in the late 1920s at the height of revolutionary reconstruction.[9] According to revolutionary leaders like Beteta, tourism offered a vehicle for economic development that fit within a broader project of nation building. Unlike land reform and agricultural ventures that emphasized the rural past, tourism would signify Mexico's entrance into the modern capitalist world. No longer isolated by revolution and endemic violence, this industry would serve as Mexico's route toward internationalism, cosmopolitanism, economic growth and development as well as improved relations with its intended market and neighbor, the United States. Still more, tourism provided the revolutionary elite with a nationalist platform that eclipsed conflicts between this industry and goals of national sovereignty, a contradiction wholly disregarded by its architects. Revolutionary nationalism so prevalent at the time would seem to work against desires to build an industry that welcomed and pandered to the foreign, especially U.S. tourists. Instead, revolutionary leaders at once professed their dedication to the nation, even bolstering nationalism, as they sold a holiday to Mexico in the image of what U.S. tourists desired and as they cooperated with American corporate and government interests.

This story illustrates much about the inner-workings of Mexico's political elites as well as relations between the revolutionary state and U.S. interests. Although Mexico's government made tourism official, its success relied on mobilized private interests to finance its development and promotion. Inextricably linked to social circles of the revolution and the revolutionary state, those individuals who built the industry with innovative ideas and national monies shared power with state institutions and became the leading spokespersons for Mexico's national image, which was marketed and sold to attract U.S. tourists. Because Mexico's tourist industry relied almost entirely on attracting these tourists who historically feared travel south of the border, revolutionary leaders employed savvy advertising strategies to refashion Mexico's reputation from an unruly to a good neighbor through stories and images in the mass media. They also sought guidance and know-how from old and new friends in the United States. At the same time, U.S. official and private interests encouraged this industry's success. Friends of Mexico and American corporate interests offered their assistance in improving Mexico's reputation by producing and disseminating promotional programs and materials throughout the United States. Likewise, the U.S. government made credible Mexico's tourist industry when it formally encouraged Americans to get to know their neighbor. These cooperative efforts between Mexicans and between Mexico and the United States served larger purposes of political consolidation, economic stability, and hemispheric solidarity. As a result, Mexico became one of the premiere playgrounds for American tourists by 1946.

The years 1928–1946 witnessed two extremes as tourism in Mexico began its transformation from afterthought to profitable national industry. For more than a decade in the early twentieth century, Mexico was mired in a bitter social revolution that took no less than two million lives. The Mexican Revolution began as a movement led by Francisco Madero to oust dictatorial figure Porfirio Díaz, and turned into an all-out battle among various interest groups to control the course of Mexico's future. On the one side were the underdogs like Pancho Villa and Emiliano Zapata who, although they lost, have been most closely linked to the myth of the revolution as a peasant uprising for land and labor rights.[10] On the other side were the more powerful middle-class leaders like Venustiano Carranza and Alvaro Obregón who fought to regain control of their nation from the privileged classes, namely the landowning elite and foreign interests. They also hoped to create a new kind of government based on democratic values such as free elections and constitutional reform.[11] When the dust settled, these victorious middle-class intellectuals, professionals, and farmers began to rebuild their nation and to consolidate their power. The revolutionary state, which emerged, appeared only partially democratic as local and national leaders handpicked their political successors from a small social circle united years later under the Institutional Revolutionary Party or PRI. Like the time of the Porfiriato (1876–1910) when the regime repressed political opposition, the revolutionary government did not share power with its challengers and, instead, co-opted labor unions and peasant groups (e.g., the Zapatistas) and often resorted to political assassination.

Despite these failings, a new government and society emerged from the Mexican Revolution both faithful to the underlying nationalist cause of building a modern nation beholden to its own people, not to foreign corporate interests or to nineteenth-century elites. Part and parcel of this new state were institutions that provided services to its citizenry such as social welfare, education, health, and job training programs as well as a stable banking system that offered savings and loan opportunities. Just as important were institutions that supported the state's cultural project to celebrate, rather than eschew, Mexico's indigenous past and to incorporate, rather than exclude, indigenous peoples from the national identity being forged. Artists like Diego Rivera were commissioned by the government to paint murals celebrating *indigenismo* (Indianness) on the walls of public buildings, and teachers were trained en masse to educate, and in effect modernize, Mexico's peasantry.[12] The revolutionary state aimed to support these new institutions through a project of economic development that ideally welcomed but did not privilege foreign capital, that did away with monopolies, and that put Mexicans on equal footing for investment opportunities.[13] The most extreme expressions of this campaign were oil, railroad, and land expropriations under Lázaro Cárdenas in the mid- to late 1930s and the more benign ones were corporate partnerships between domestic and international capital (e.g., Hualera Euzkadi and B.F. Goodrich) that functioned to limit foreign dominance of specific industries in Mexico.[14]

With few resources of its own, the Mexican revolutionary state continued to rely on external sources of investment, on foreign technology, and on a small, emerging group of revolutionary elites with capital to invest. It should come as no surprise then that by the late 1920s the winners of the revolution,[15] who only years earlier had been on or behind the scenes of battlefields and who had fought to free Mexico from an unelected president believed to have catered to foreign business interests, sat down at conference tables to discuss, of all things, tourism. They debated slogans that sold Mexico as a vacation destination and encouraged Americans over the radio and in print to become friends with their southern neighbor. Some of these men would even venture to Hollywood to meet with celebrities and film producers who, in turn, acted out holidaymaking to Mexico for ordinary Americans to follow. This examination of tourism, then, sheds some light on the uneasy balance between economic development and nationalism, between this capitalist venture and revolutionary rhetoric, and between the government, Mexican capital, and American business interests.

This study begins when the government formally recognized tourism's potential profit and began to study, organize, develop, and promote it after 1928. In contrast to the Porfiriato (1876–1911), when businessmen and the government worked to lure visitors for the purpose of investment in a particular industry, the revolutionary elite—government officials and private investors—by the late 1920s, sought profits from the tourist who spent his or her holiday in

Mexico.[16] As early as 1927, the federal government formally expressed its dedication to and involvement in the development of tourism. Passage of unprecedented migration policies that regulated entry and exit through Mexico's then loose borders and ports identified the new category of "tourist," as well as the need to provide services and impose restrictions on this group. By 1928, the federal government took its first organizational step by creating the Pro-Tourism Commission (CPT), an agency within the Ministry of Interior formed by members of the Migration, Health, and Customs Departments who studied and recommended necessary steps to create a successful tourist industry. Less than a year later, the government reorganized the CPT into the Mixed Pro-Tourism Commission (CMPT). Recognizing that they could not make a successful tourist industry alone, government officials called on representatives from the private sector to cooperate in promoting their nation's natural beauty and in developing a tourist infrastructure. After 1928, revolutionary elites from the state and private groups dedicated themselves to developing and promoting tourism. They initiated studies, organized meetings and conferences, improved and constructed new modes of transportation, licensed and regulated hotels and restaurants, preserved tourist attractions, protected "national treasures," and debated the creation of new ones. During these formative years, the tourist industry yelped from growing pains. Poor organization, little profit, few tourists, economic depression, bad press, and political chaos hindered its growth from 1928 until the beginning of World War II. But, in the years immediately following World War II, nearly 20 years of work toward the building of this industry paid off with high profits and high tourist rates, and resulted more broadly in a transformed capital city and nation.

This study also starts to make sense of the intricate web of social and political elites who coalesced around tourism as a patriotic and profitable industry. It identifies the relationships between these prominent, civic-minded, and often self-interested members of countless public and private organizations who believed that tourism would make Mexico a modern, world contender. It also analyzes the rhetoric used to justify the development of an industry that seemed to negate, but in fact bolstered, revolutionary nationalism. This study ends when the success begins. That is, it concludes when tourism flourished and when its pioneers finally reaped substantial rewards. By the 1950s the face of tourism had become professionalized and big business. Studies have erroneously credited Miguel Alemán, president from 1946 to 1952 and Acapulco developer, for this shift. Charged with being a playboy and corrupt politician, he is also popularly recognized as the architect and father of tourism in Mexico.[17] In fact, most Mexican publications about tourism demarcate the industry's birth in 1947 with the first federal tourist law written by Alemán.[18] Yet, as this study shows, Alemán certainly modernized but was hardly the mastermind behind the industry that began years before his position as Interior minister (1940–1945) or as president. With this in mind, this study does not organize its analysis around the traditional *sexenio* (six-year presidential term) approach because no single president or administration was responsible for its ebbs and flows. Like any other industry, tourism relied on the condition of both seller and buyer, which in large part, has always been determined by the market. Its ups and downs have everything to do with economic, political, and social conditions within Mexico, the United States, and the world. The chapters that follow examine these highs and lows of tourism organized around local, national, and international events to give the reader a sense of the roller coaster on which Mexico's tourist industry rode. Whereas chapters 1, 2, and 3 focus primarily on tourist development, chapters 4 and 5 examine its promotion.

* * *

It only seems fair to provide a brief warning about the definitions and boundaries of this book. First, this is an examination of an elite-driven industry aimed to attract the most profitable vacationer at the time, the American tourist. National tourism is only briefly mentioned because the historical actors themselves rarely discussed its benefit during the years 1928–1946. Without question, domestic tourism existed. In fact, many of the revolutionary leaders who developed tourism had traveled throughout Mexico or had lived extensively abroad. There is also a long history of the well-to-do from Mexico City vacationing in places like Cuernavaca and Lake Chapala. Nevertheless, American tourists, whose spending power far outweighed that of Mexicans, were the industry's prime target.

Second, while this is a study about Mexican history, first, it is also a study about tourism and the way it suggests new possibilities for analyzing the making of modern Mexico. Although relatively new to the field of Mexican history,[19] this study of tourism fits into the growing scholarship of tourist studies forged by social scientists in the 1970s.[20] Pioneering tourist scholar Valene Smith defines a tourist as "a temporarily leisured person who voluntarily visits a place away from home for the purposes of experiencing a change"[21] while Hal Rothman defines tourism as "an activity through which masses of people experience places other than their homes in a system of institutions designed to convey them on their journey in whatever degree of comfort or privation they choose."[22] This freedom to choose that tourists enjoy, Rothman continues, is a product of industrialization and consumerism just as modern tourism itself emerged from "the wealth, the time, the conceptual need . . . and the opportunity to visit places that soon catered to [peoples'] taste."[23] John Urry's work, especially his exploration of the "tourist gaze," informs much of this study. He argues that tourists choose to frequent, or in his words gaze upon, specific tourist attractions based on what they anticipate to be different from as well as familiar to their own reality. This gaze, reinforced by images in the mass media, is reconstructed by tourist professionals who aim to package and sell said attraction based on what Urry calls a "collection of signs."[24] In other words, like all products, the way in which tourist sites are marketed fit with preconceived snapshots held by its targeted audience: the Indian with sombrero, the sandy beach with palm tree, the Hawaiian woman in hula skirt. In the case of Mexico, as explored in this study, it becomes particularly interesting that tourist professionals disseminated new imagery in the U.S. mass media in order to change the tourist gaze while they simultaneously sustained the gaze they tried to change.

Defined in a variety of ways, tourism here is understood as the sum of its many parts: the tourist trade as a business and the tourist as a leisured person. Of course, inherent in this complex topic are countless windows of analysis that this study takes up but may not fully explore. Some of these include the act of and motivations for travel, the interactions between guest and host, the tourist professionals who promote a holiday destination and thus make it desirable to the potential tourist, the tourist developers who build an infrastructure of highways, hotels, airports, and other services to meet the demands of guests, and the service workers who mix drinks, check in guests at hotel receptions, clean rooms, and give tours. This analysis of tourism also begins to explore the host of historical actors who brokered the act of holidaymaking including statesmen, businesspeople, service workers, travel agents, celebrities, artists, writers, journalists, and travelers; it is their participation in tourism that shapes the success or failure of a destination. It is also their motivations, intentions, and actions that beg for scholarly analysis. Still more, this study illustrates the relationship between tourism and nation-states in a broader international system. Because it is inherently linked to economics, politics, national boundaries, immigration policies, and even national identity, tourism is an industry and product that is susceptible to changes in domestic and world markets as well as relations among nations who are all part of the broader international system. Thus, conditions within a nation or between nation-states can directly affect the viability of and profits from tourism.[25] Finally, tourism reveals transformations because it entails power. Like all products, the offerings of a holiday destination must meet the demands of discerning guests. Hotels provide amenities to which guests are accustomed, whether it is color television with cable, a bidet, or air conditioning. Nations provide modern highways, train stations, and airports to make travel conditions convenient and easy. Good, bad, or indifferent, in the course of accommodating one's target market, the host country, city, or community is inevitably altered. For example, new venues like nightclubs built to accommodate and attract tourists might be frequented by local elites, or familiar foods offered as a courtesy to guests unaccustomed to regional spices might be incorporated into the local diet.

Given the multifaceted nature of tourism as a subject, this study does not claim to exhaust all research possibilities. It focuses instead on three themes: the relationship between tourist development, modernization, and Mexico's revolutionary government; the methods by which tourist professionals, mainly social and political elites from government ministries and private industry, recast their nation's image in the United States from a lawless, bandit, rural nation to a civilized, modern, urban one; and tourism's transforming effect from infrastructure and cultural practice to Mexico's broader relations with the United States. This work forms only one part of a growing scholarly field and hopes to inspire others to examine its implications.

CHAPTER 1

MEXICO'S NEW REVOLUTION: THE RACE FOR THE TOURIST DOLLAR, 1928–1929

Since the end of World War I, Cuba and Canada enjoyed multimillion dollar profits from U.S. tourists. Motorists crossed their northern border with ease in search of outdoor activities such as fishing, skiing, and hunting while others ferried to the nearest tropical island of Cuba in search of debauchery and spectacle—beaches, gambling, floor-shows, and bars. Yet U.S. tourists rarely ventured beyond their southern borders and into the heart of their most contentious neighbor, Mexico. Unlike Cuba or Canada, Mexico experienced a long history of strained political and cultural relations with the United States dating as far back as the mid-nineteenth century when the two went to war (1846–1848) and, as a result, Mexico lost almost half its national territory in the Treaty of Guadalupe Hidalgo. Moreover, unlike its neighbors, Mexico had only begun to emerge from the physical and spiritual destruction caused by the revolution from 1910 to 1920 and by religious rebellion from 1926 to 1929.

Just as the violence subsided, as revolutionary leaders consolidated political power under the National Revolutionary Party (PNR), and as relations with the United States improved,[1] President Portes Gil declared during a press conference in 1929 that Mexico intended to enter the race for the tourist dollar. To lure the tourist dollar south, the president, according to the *New York Times*, ordered all officials at its borders and ports to help make travel to Mexico easy and safe. He also told private enterprises that they should cooperate in the development of infrastructure by constructing tourist accommodations and services.[2] As proof to U.S. tourists that Mexico finally enjoyed peace and stability and was ready for visitors, the president planned to decrease the number of military personnel who policed trains in an effort to ensure the safety of visitors.[3] Finally, the capstone of his said program came when the president announced that the government had created its first official tourist organization, the Mixed Pro-Tourism Commission (CMPT), codified into law on July 6. Unlike its short-lived predecessor the Pro-Tourism Commission (CPT), created six months earlier with officials from Customs, Health, and Migration Departments for the study and recommendation of border policies, the CMPT brought together representatives from related government ministries and private businesses who, bound by a firm belief that tourism offered Mexico the route toward progress, would devote their energies entirely to building this national industry.

For Mexico to stand a chance against regional competitors, tourist pioneers, most who were prominent members of the revolutionary elite or what scholar Frank Brandenburg has referred to as the "Revolutionary Family,"[4] had to first understand the competition, the judges, and the players involved in this tourist race. Only then did they begin to organize a team composed of official and private members. Through careful study of tourist industries around the world, Mexico began to carve its niche within the confines of overarching revolutionary goals. Most notably, leaders argued for economic development funded by Mexican capital and molded by Mexican hands, the same creed that guided nation-building projects from 1925 to 1946. Unfortunately, because Mexico's government decided to forge a tourist industry at the onset of a worldwide economic depression, the industry did not noticeably grow from 1928 to 1935. Nevertheless, those interested in developing tourism did more than spin their wheels. They used these years effectively to pinpoint the main ingredients that made a successful tourist industry and began to train for the long haul.

Not surprising, the president's announcement that the state would develop tourism came on the heels of crucial events that placed Mexico in the international spotlight. Charles Lindbergh flew his famous goodwill flight to Mexico in 1927 (where he fell in love with the U.S. ambassador's daughter Anne). U.S. Ambassador Dwight D. Morrow helped negotiate the terms that ended nearly four years of church-state conflict during the Cristero Rebellion. And, reelected president, Alvaro Obregón, was assassinated on the eve of his inauguration. It also followed international events that gradually had debilitated

Europe's tourist industry during these interwar years. The political and economic climate in Europe—destruction from World War I and rise of fascism and nationalist socialism—encouraged competition in the western hemisphere and shaped a new desire among U.S. tourists to "rediscover America." Mexico's promise of progress and development after the revolution, coupled with the possibilities for a working relationship with the United States and opportunities to take over markets that war-torn Europe could no longer command, ushered in a new era of hope.

For the next two decades, revolutionary leaders worked to centralize political power, to build a strong state, to strengthen the economy, and to unify the nation. Tourism was an integral part of this transition to peace and progress. Because Mexico's ability to attract U.S. tourists determined its success, tourism functioned as a barometer for national development. The gradual increase, with some declines, in the number of tourists entering Mexico from 1929 to 1946 reflected the nation's relative stability and perceptions of its stability.[5] Even the slightest suspicion or malicious rumor spread in the U.S. press about the possibility of revolution or rebellion during presidential elections affected tourist rates almost immediately. Tourist rates also mirrored Mexico's advancements especially in highway[6] and hotel construction. Finally, this increase illustrated progress in labor, namely an emerging urban-based service sector such as the trained and licensed tour guides, hotel clerks, waiters, and travel agents.

Tourist numbers and profits not only reflected progress and peace, but efforts to develop the industry also helped build national unity. Because its success relied on attracting tourists to national treasures— its vast beaches, colonial monuments, archaeological ruins, and cosmopolitan capital city—tourism inherently evoked pride in things uniquely Mexican. When the federal government first called on private enterprise and local groups to help develop tourism it did so by emphasizing that Mexico's natural beauty, its history, and its cultural traditions were undoubtedly enough to attract large numbers of tourists.[7] As a result, officials and private individuals at the national and local levels, who formed groups to foment tourism, beamed with pride in their nation's attributes, writing that it far exceeded what tourists would find in Asia, Europe, Cuba, or Canada. Others worked to preserve their nation's artistic and historical heritage. The federal government passed its first laws to protect colonial monuments and Mesoamerican pyramids.[8] Municipal officials in Taxco and Pátzcuaro passed the first regulations to preserve *lo típico*—its typical, colonial character.[9]

Tourism also offered a partial solution to Mexico's severe economic problems. By the late 1920s, national production and export of metals decreased by 38 percent while the value of oil exports plummeted.[10] The widening gap between what the nation earned from exports and what it spent on imports made it more difficult for the government to make payments on its foreign debt. This situation prevented any immediate chance for the government to regain international credit. The minister of finance, and future tourist pioneer, Luis Montes de Oca, wrote that Mexico had gained political independence in the nineteenth century, but it had failed to break free from colonial ties. Mexico's economy, he argued, was based on the production of primary materials whose supply depended on foreign demands. Montes de Oca saw the solution to economic dependency in the development of new national industries by Mexicans and for Mexicans.[11] Tourism seemed the best solution to his recommendation. Characterized as an "invisible export," tourists spent money on attractions in Mexico, but their money and the product theoretically remained in Mexico. It presented an efficient way to increase profits without increasing imports, thus, helping to balance its international payments. Coined by leaders as an economic solution and one that served broader state-building goals of economic development and national unity, tourism appeared both the logical remedy and great hurdle. When government officials declared their intention to enter the race for the tourist dollar in 1928 the Department of National Statistics had recorded the entry of a measly 12,586 foreign tourists in Mexico, a third of whom reached Mexico City. Meanwhile, that same year, an estimated 80,000 tourists sought pleasure and relaxation in Cuba where they had spent over US$29 million.[12]

How would Mexico join the race? Officials quickly discovered that the answers lie beyond Mexico's immediate tourist attractions. Prominent journalist and *El Universal* founder, Felix F. Palavicini, bluntly stated to the nation in a 1930 radio program that two revolutions, three presidents, and an attempted assassination against the president in the last four years had created an international reputation for violence in Mexico and an atmosphere of distrust.[13] Worse still, the Interior Ministry received complaints from tourists who could not find a single lavatory along the just-completed, 151-mile section of the highway to Mexico City, from Laredo-Monterrey.[14] Finally, U.S. hotelier Frank A. Dudley, reported to the heads of railway companies and President Ortíz Rubio that Mexico had few hotels appealing to the middle-income American and none for upper-class travelers.[15]

Mexico's violent reputation in the United States and its lack of tourist accommodations were two prevailing problems contemplated by tourist pioneers throughout the next decade. Yet, participants still found one of their greatest challenges rooted in nationalism: how to reconcile the sale of a pleasure holiday to Mexico without selling out the revolution's goals. Amid broader efforts to define *lo mexicano* (Mexicanness) during the 1920s through education, art, archaeology, and music, tourism emerged as another opportunity for revolutionary leaders to define, negotiate, and preserve national identity. To garner support for this industry and to justify the sale of Mexico's tourist attractions, policy makers, bankers, hoteliers, and others responsible for teasing out the kinks during these formative years, deployed patriotic language, national symbolism, and protectionist policies. Economic and cultural nationalism expressed by tourist developers, at least rhetorically, guided the industry until after World War II, when tourism helped balance the nation's payments and became big business.

THE COMPETITORS

In an effort to determine what Mexico needed to compete in the race for the tourist dollar, government officials asked Mexican diplomats around the world to study and report on the tourism industries in the areas under their jurisdiction. On the basis of these reports, even before any institutional organization took place, Mexico's government weighed and measured the potential gains—profits and progress— and losses—domestic control over national development—posed by this kind of vulnerable industry. Even before this request had been made, consul generals were possibly the first to write about the potential demand for the development of Mexico's tourist industry. As early as 1924, E. Ferreira from his post in San Diego, California, reported on a recent rise at his consulate in tourist inquiries into the climate, hotels, and attractions in Mexico City, Guadalajara, Hermosillo, Monterrey, Mazatlán, and Guaymas. Much to his dismay, he was unable to provide any such information because his office lacked published materials. He expressed hope that Chambers of Commerce and hotel owners in these cities follow the lead of those in San Diego and Los Angeles whose descriptive brochures had made California's tourist industry a success.[16] Mexico's consul general in Havana, José Damaso Fernández, reported on the large profits made from tourism on the island. In only one month during the winter season, December 25– January 26, tourists spent no less than US$6 million. He attributed this in large part to the recent organization of Cuba's National Tourism

Commission (to which private businesses donated US$250,000), and to the imaginative public works projects, especially the nearly complete Grand Central Highway. Mexico's ability to offer the tourist its "valued treasures," he argued, relied on the rapid expansion of its highways.[17]

Over the next few years, the reports on tourism received by the Ministry of Foreign Affairs proved invaluable for organizing, developing, and promoting Mexico's future tourist industry. In June 1928, the Ministry of Foreign Affairs asked its representatives abroad to write a formal report based on the following eight questions:

What is the importance and magnitude of tourism?
What kinds of tourists visit?
What system of propaganda is used to attract tourism?
What are the benefits of tourism?
What are the prejudices or problems of tourism?
What methods are used to avoid undesirable tourists?
What action does shipping and railway companies, Chambers of
    Commerce and financial institutions take to foment and regulate
    tourism?
What action does the government take to foment and regulate
    tourism?[18]

Among the most valuable reports, were those from Prague, Phoenix, St. Louis, Chicago, Galveston and Del Rio, Texas, Canada, and Cuba. While Cuba and Canada became the most studied models, other locations offered interesting examples of the relationship between government and private institutions, about the way a city sold itself to tourists, about the kinds of attractions Mexico could develop, about the importance of propaganda, and, above all, about what U.S. tourists deemed pleasurable. For example, Consul General A.V. Martínez, posted in Phoenix, reported that between 1910 and 1927 profits from tourism had risen from US$4 million to US$33 million in that city due in large part to the initiative taken by state and local governments in constructing highways that united Phoenix to neighboring cities and tourist sites (that brought in 800,000 motor tourists in 1927 alone), as well as the federal government's interest in building and maintaining sanatoriums for tuberculosis victims and others suffering from respiratory illnesses. Yet, Martínez emphasized, the transportation companies produced and distributed tourism information signifying that their booming industry relied on genuine cooperation between businessmen, bankers, and government officials.[19] In

St. Louis where tourists generally came to see its parks, monuments, libraries, and universities, Consul General A. Casarín found that there, too, the railway companies, hoteliers, and other private groups produced tourist propaganda and disseminated it through mail and radio, while the state government spent over US$75 million on the construction and conservation of highways.[20]

Other reports offered different stories. In Chicago, for example, where the main attractions were tall buildings, cultural centers, factories, sports fields, and theatres, tourism relied primarily on visits by conventioneers, businessmen, and industrialists. Mexican Consul General Luis Lupián reported that Chicago held roughly 780 conventions that brought in over one million visitors. These conventions proved beneficial to the city where private business was responsible for nearly all the development and promotion of tourism including the opening of tourist offices in hotel lobbies and in transportation offices.[21] Ismael S. Vázquez reported that in his jurisdiction, Galveston, Texas, where beach resorts and spas attracted only local tourists, an international women's bathing beauty contest was organized each year by local businesses to attract foreign tourists, which has, in turn, increased the demand for hotel construction and increased sales at restaurants. In the border town of Del Rio, Texas, Consul L. Peña wrote that although border residents generally took advantage of the rivers and creeks near the Villa Acuña, each year a small number of prominent Americans drove there to spend an estimated US$7 per person each day on the consumption of alcohol and on the purchase of fishing licenses, souvenirs, local tour guides, and cooks.[22]

Consular reports from Europe, especially those of Edmundo González Roa from Prague, told of a similar kind of tourism industry. González wrote that Czechoslovakia's industry attracted about 444,000 tourists in 1927 with the help of Chambers of Commerce that organized commercial fairs and expositions, state-owned shipping and railway companies that produced and disseminated tourist propaganda, and travel agencies like Cook Tours that produced radio advertisements and provided tourist assistance and organized excursions. Meanwhile, government agents handled all issues pertaining to immigration as well as the construction and maintenance of highways. As for the most desired tourist, González reported that Czechoslovakia preferred Americans because they spent the most money in the least amount of time.[23]

Together, the reports made by Mexican consuls directed officials to some of the main ingredients that made successful tourism industries: dedication and cooperation between government institutions, transportation companies, and private businesses; mass production of promotional tourist information and widespread dissemination in hotels and transportation offices and over the radio; and the development of tourist attractions like beach resorts, spas, and fishing spots as well as convention centers to attract all types of U.S. tourists. In fact, Mexico's tourist pioneers considered the facets just described and factored them into the niche they carved for Mexico during the late 1920s.

Additional reports on Canada and Cuba submitted to the Ministry of Foreign Affairs by consuls and others, echoed these elements and provided special insights based on their geographical and geopolitical proximity to the United States and their common target audience, the U.S. tourist. Reports on Canada found that 60 percent of all visiting U.S. tourists arrived by automobile and that the two to three million motor tourists who arrived between the years 1926 and 1927 spent an estimated US$106–US$120 million.[24] Canada offered the tourist beautiful scenery, fishing, hunting, skiing, and other outdoor activities. Nevertheless, one report attributed its success to the ease with which U.S. motorists passed rapidly and painlessly through border crossings for a period up to six months without paying a customs duty or showing a passport.[25] That motor tourists entered Canada with few requirements seemed a far cry from what motorists faced when they entered Mexico, especially through Nuevo Laredo, the most popular border entry once the Nuevo Laredo-Mexico City Highway was under construction. Passport requirements were discarded by 1928, but immigration officials required tourists first to apply for a tourist card at their local Mexican Consulate or at the Laredo Chamber of Commerce, to pay a Mex$1 or Mex$2 fee for the card, to show proof of vaccinations, and, finally, to post a bond on their car equal to import duties. These requirements, many of which were done away with by the time of the inauguration of the Nuevo Laredo-Mexico City Highway in 1936, in part explain why an average of only 315 motor tourists a month entered Mexico through Nuevo Laredo in 1929.[26] To increase entry rates, improvements around automobile entry into Mexico became top priority for government officials and private associations alike.

If Canada provided a model for international motor travel, Cuba demonstrated the extreme—the best and the worst—of a tourist industry. While popular opinion praised Cuba for its tourist accomplishments, others told of a much darker side. Those who praised the island's success focused on its profits, its sophisticated promotional literature and transportation systems, and the urban renewal projects that had transformed Havana. According to one Mexican official, Cuba offered tourists a holiday in a hygienic, modern, and elegant atmosphere. By this he meant that tourists could rent cars without being abused because the state regulated the prices. Tourists could get around by "clean, ample, esthetic and comfortable" buses. Havana was clean with no beggars to be found while its nightclubs, casinos, and other diversions brought in close to US$3,000 per day, and offered tourists never-ending fun. Finally, he reported, Havana had its own English-speaking, specially uniformed brigade of police officers who offered assistance to tourists and who guaranteed their safety.[27]

Despite these advances, Mexico's consul general in Havana, Manuel Álvarez, described the dark side of Cuba's successful tourist industry. Indeed, tourism in Havana was extraordinary: the city had been improved, highways, railways, and hotels had been constructed, new jobs had been created, and the Cuban currency appeared stable. Yet, he argued, Havana's tourist industry was not a benefit to the nation because foreigners, mostly U.S. investors, owned its hotels, cabarets, automobile dealerships, casinos, race tracks, resorts, and transportation companies. As a result, Álvarez argued, U.S. tourists did little for the island's economy because their money fell into the pockets of foreigners, not Cubans. Contrary to popular opinion, he wrote, Cuban currency did not exist, what with Cuba's loss of land, industry, commerce, and banking one only found thousands of bills marked, "made in the U.S.A." He concluded his report by stating that he hoped Mexico's tourist developers would learn from Cuba's mistakes and would ensure that all services developed and all profits made from tourism remain in Mexican hands.[28]

Mexico's tourist pioneers had much to learn from Álvarez's report that equated Cuban tourism to a loss of national sovereignty. But whereas Cuba's quest for independence from foreign holdings would not come until 1956, Mexican leaders had already begun to build anew, after its own fight to take control of land, railroads, and natural resources that had previously been held in foreign hands. Efforts to construct, direct, and control new national industries in revolutionary Mexico remained a principal goal for official and private groups throughout the 1920s and 1930s. But while a principle goal, control over tourism was neither an easy task nor a realistic one given the nature of its development and promotion. Although steadfast to the revolution and, thus, the national cause, Mexico's tourist pioneers—its government officials, politicians, bankers, engineers, hoteliers, and businessmen—often conflated state projects with personal interests. Still more, like Cuba and countless other desirable destinations, something inherently gets lost in the interaction between host and guest. In the case of Mexico, as this study argues, tourist development helped shape a new society of modernity from mass urbanization and consumption to professionalized service and transportation industries so much so that contemporary Mexican writers like Octavio Paz and José Emilio Pacheco would eventually lament the loss of Mexican values by the 1950s.

THE TEAM

The Mexican consular reports suggested the ingredients for a successful tourist industry—infrastructure, public–private cooperation and promotion—but it did not provide directions for its organization and construction. Mexico's government spent much of its time forming commissions charged with devising a plan. What began as an impromptu Pro-Tourism Commission (CPT) that met to standardize and ease the requirements for tourists at the Mexico-U.S. border in 1928, was followed by utter chaos.[29] During the *Maximato*, from 1928 to 1934, tourism was organized and reorganized under a variety of commissions including the CPT, the CMPT, and the National Tourism Commission (CNT), mirroring the equally chaotic political climate.[30] Luckily, other groups emerged to pick up where government organizations failed to start. Members of these private associations demonstrated the real strength of Mexico's team by forming a network of interests among government officials and private enterprise.

One of the first and most prominent sponsors of tourist development in Mexico was led by Alberto Mascareñas, director general of the recently founded Banco de México, S.A. (Bank of Mexico), who created a Department of Tourism in April 1928. Mascareñas announced on April 15 that the bank planned to cooperate with government agencies as well as transportation, hotel, and commercial businesses in attracting tourists to Mexico.[31] While never explicitly stated, he created the bank's Department of Tourism in preparation for the completed section of Mexico's first international highway from Nuevo Laredo-Monterrey, which was to be ready by early 1929. Under the charge of Antonio L. Rodríguez, one very determined, salaried employee who was former consul in London currently working for the bank in Monterrey, the department in just four years and on a limited budget (around Mex$8,242 per year) became Mexico's first publicity agent. In 1929, Rodríguez and Mascareñas produced an English-language descriptive brochure entitled, "Visit Mexico the Land of Beauty and Romance," that promoted Mexico City as the ideal tourist attraction. In this fairly lengthy and costly brochure that included photographs and a foldout map of Mexico City, one finds descriptions of things to see and do in the capital and in its outlying suburbs and towns. It also published lists of services provided by the bank including the purchase of Bank of Mexico Travelers Checks and tourist postal services.[32] Later that same year, they produced another English-language brochure that introduced former and future students of the National University's Summer School for Foreigners to the possibility of learning and vacationing in Mexico City.[33] And, in 1932, they worked directly with government ministries to write an English-language guide entitled, "How to Enter Mexico." Geared toward motor tourists, the brochure provided a list of all regulations related to border entry as well as descriptive sections on modes of transportation and contacts while in Mexico.[34]

Because the bank's primary interests lie in the promotion of Mexico in the United States, the government invited Rodríguez and Mascareñas to represent the Bank of Mexico at meetings held between 1929 and 1932 by government organizations like the CPT, CMPT, and CNT. At one CMPT meeting, Mascareñas announced the bank's plans to broadcast a weekly radio show in English to Americans entitled, "Mexico Nights." This program would present popular music, folklore songs, military bands, and short talks designed to impress upon listeners the advantages of travel to Mexico.[35] He even suggested that the CMPT devise some catchy slogans to be repeated throughout the program such as "Visit Mexico—The Egypt of the Americas—A Foreign Land a Step Away"; "Have You Ever Heard of Mexico?—Ask Mr. and Mrs. Lindbergh—They Know All About It"; "From Dawn to Sunset Every Day New Miles are Added to our Highways—You Can Drive Now from Laredo to Monterrey and Ciudad Victoria—Within a Year You Will be Able to Motor All the Way Down to Mexico City."[36] By 1931, Mascareñas hired three additional employees who devised innovative ways to promote tourism in Mexico. One of the most interesting methods employed by the department included the production of stamps embossed with images of Mexico's tourist attractions. The bank sent each Mexican Consulate around the world 500 stamps to be used for postage.[37]

The Bank of Mexico's Tourist Department only functioned for four years before its founder had to resign in disgrace after butting heads with *jefe máximo* (absolute leader), Plutarco Elías Calles, who was pulling the presidential strings.[38] When Mascareñas resigned in 1932 and his successor cancelled the department, their initial labor in the promotion of Mexico's tourist industry was not forgotten and it set precedence for the profound role that the Bank of Mexico would play in promoting and financing tourism by the mid-1930s under its future director Luis Montes de Oca.[39] First, Rodríguez and Mascareñas established patterns for some major trends in tourist promotion and propaganda. By the mid-1930s, successors followed their example and used radio as well as slogans to promote Mexico in the United States. Second, while Mascareñas disappeared from historical record, Antonio L. Rodríguez remained active in Monterrey, where he dedicated much of his career to the development and promotion of motor tourism. And finally, these initial efforts guaranteed the Bank of Mexico a place in the starting line up for Mexico's future development of tourism.

Another agency to emerge in conjunction with the Bank of Mexico's Department of Tourism was the Mexican Tourism Association (MTA) located in New York City.[40] Members of the MTA celebrated their first meeting in late November 1928 on Liberty Street in Manhattan. Those who joined the celebration included agents from National Railways of Mexico (FFCCN), Mexican Railways, and South Pacific of Mexico; a representative from Pullman Company; a steamship company agent from the N.Y. & Cuba S.S. Co.; representatives from the travel agencies of Thomas Cook & Son and Henry Tours, Inc.; president of the Southwestern Passenger Association; president of the Trunk Line Association; a representative from the Mexican Consulate; the manager of the Hotel Waldorf Astoria; and a representative from the Mexican Chamber of Commerce in New York.[41] Because transportation companies and other businesses related to tourist services founded the MTA, its primary interest was to work with the government to standardize immigration requirements, which would facilitate entry into Mexico for railway and steamship passengers and for members of organized tour groups. Only a week before their first meeting, José M. Bejarano, secretary of the Mexican Chamber of Commerce in New York, had witnessed Mexican immigration agents take two hours to check the luggage of only four people. He noted that the agents were not uniformed, that they carried rifles, and that they clearly abused tourists by charging tariffs on personal items. To make matters worse, he noticed that the border station in Nuevo Laredo did not offer toilet facilities.[42] Bejarano's observations were summarily included in the association's agenda that called on the government to devise a protocol for luggage regulations and inspections at Mexico's border.

The power of the MTA to shape Mexican policy was nothing at which to scoff. Andrés Landa y Piña, later CMPT secretary, noted that the MTA's suggestions pushed government officials to create its first tourist commission in 1928 as proof that they had begun to provide and improve tourist facilities.[43] But when asked what Mexico needed to foment tourism, Landa responded that while the government was doing their part, it was the public's responsibility to provide tourist amenities such as hotels and restaurants. Without cooperation between the government and public, he argued, an increase in tourism would be impossible.[44] In contrast, members of the private sector, including those of the MTA, argued that the government had done little up to that point to develop tourism save for a series of immigration laws passed in 1903 that sought to curb the entrance of undesirables, namely Japanese and Chinese immigrants, and migration laws in 1926–1927 that began to classify, record, and restrict persons entering Mexico by creating categories for immigrants and for visitors.[45] But as the Nuevo Laredo-Monterrey section of the Pan-American Highway neared completion, neither government nor private sectors had the time to debate responsibility. Indeed, the moment had arrived for Mexico to organize its team to develop tourism.

The urgency to coordinate efforts shaped the emergence of the government's first official tourist organization, the Mixed Pro-Tourism Committee (CMPT), as well as the privately founded Mexican American Automobile Association (AAMA). Established in January 1929 on the initiative of the National Road Commission and the Bank of Mexico, the AAMA brought together Mexican and American members of the Inter-American Highway Association (a group responsible for helping to organize funds for the construction of the Nuevo Laredo-Mexico City Highway) as they returned from an American Road Builders Association meeting in Cleveland, Ohio. At a banquet held in the St. Anthony Hotel, in San Antonio, Texas, participants formally created the AAMA.[46] Known three years later simply as the Mexican Automobile Association (AMA), its members became the premier developers of motor tourism throughout the 1930s. Most notably, however, the AAMA united official and private sectors in Mexico, as well as interested U.S. groups, for the broader purpose of fomenting tourism. At their first meeting held on January 8, 1929, members named Antonio L. Rodríguez (representative from the Bank of Mexico) president, William H. Furlong (representative from the International Highway Association) American secretary, José Rivera R. (representative from the National Road Commission) Mexican secretary, and Charles Mumm (representative from the American Automobile Association) border representative. When members of the AAMA met again in April to draw up recommendations for the CPT, the Nuevo Laredo-Monterrey section of Mexico's first international highway was ready for motorists. Their suggestions drew the state's attention to the importance of motor travel as the most preferred form among Americans who lived for the freedom of driving and who purchased automobiles at a rapidly increasing rate.[47] With the expected rise in U.S. motor tourists along Mexico's first international highway, the AAMA recommended that the state increase the gasoline tax to finance future construction on this and other highways, a tax later imposed when the Nuevo Laredo-Mexico City Highway opened in 1936. And, as a way to simplify procedures at the border they recommended that the guaranty requirement be cancelled and that Chambers of Commerce along border cities be allowed to expedite the required paperwork and grant passage to motor travelers.

By the time President Portes Gil announced the creation of the CMPT in July 1929, the AAMA had been planning an important meeting to be held in Monterrey on August 7–8, which ultimately served as the premiere opportunity for representatives from private and official sectors to publicly demonstrate their support for the development of tourism. Attendees included prominent government officials like Nuevo León's Governor Aarón Sáenz Garza, representatives from the Industry and Commerce and Foreign Affairs Ministries, and Chamber of Commerce representatives from San Antonio, Nuevo Laredo, Laredo, Monterrey, Saltillo, Brownsville, and other border cities. More than just a meeting to draw up the association's official constitution, association members used the opportunity to pledge their cooperation with the state by naming President Portes Gil and other official CMPT representatives as honorary AAMA members.[48] In return, the state's clear presence at the meeting and support for the AAMA equally signified that with cooperation from the private sector, tourism was indeed Mexico's best hope for progress.

In addition to private associations dedicated to tourism, the government did their part to discuss ways to foment private interests when President Calles founded the CPT in 1928. Participants from the CPT spent most of their energies trying to figure out exactly how to organize themselves, and made little progress during the commission's short life. At its first meeting on December 27, 1928, the Interior Ministry invited representatives from three government departments—Migration, Customs, and Health—to address the issues of border restrictions set forth by the MTA only a month before. Over the next few months CPT members, many of whom also sat on the AAMA, submitted reports for review. Their recommendations included detailed lists of suggested personal belongings allowed in tourists' luggage, which allowed men to bring only one evening suit and five hats, and women two evening suits and one parasol,[49] as well as procedures for border agents to follow if a visitor with signs of a transmittable disease tried to enter Mexico.[50] Suggestions from the Bank of Mexico's Antonio L. Rodríguez on behalf of the Migration Section included the proposition that the category of "tourist" be defined as one who arrives in Mexico exclusively for pleasure. As such, he argued, they should receive free tourist cards.[51] Under the direction of Landa y Piña, the commission even published its first and only bilingual tourist magazine entitled, *"México" guia de turismo* ("Mexico" Tourist Guide) in an effort to change impressions about Mexico in the United States and at home.[52] Essays included descriptions of national highway construction, railroad schedules and fares, and information on things to do in Mexico City, Taxco, Puebla, and Guanajuato as well as detailed plans for the construction of a resort hotel in Baja California.

Only a few months after its inception, one commission member complained that they lacked a plan with clarity and depth.[53] His comment set the tone for the rest of the meeting, and members outlined what they believed a tourist organization should do. Although their sketch resembled the presidential decree that authorized the eventual CMPT, his comment symbolized a much larger visionary problem and slowed any advancement over the next few months. Once the president did announce the formation of the Pro-Tourism Commission, which caused quite a fuss in the Mexican and U.S. press, members did little more than discuss its reorganization. And by November, members of the CMPT discussed their plans to change the organization's personality, and name, from the CMPT to the National Tourism Commission (CNT). This, many argued, would give the organization legal power so that it could receive donations, government subsidies, tax exemptions as well as open its own offices. Just before he left office in December, President Portes Gil signed the law that created the CNT, ushering another change in name that only retarded any real progress.[54]

* * *

Even before the government created an official tourist organization, progress had already been made without its direct help. The Bank of Mexico, the MTA, the AAMA, the CPT, and local Pro-Tourism groups[55] had emerged and had already begun to establish ties and to forge relationships between private and official institutions in Mexico and the United States. In addition, world-renowned travel agencies, Wagons-Lits & Thomas Cook and Sons, accepted the National Bank of Mexico's invitation when it opened for business in Mexico City on June 19, 1929. Why, then, did the CMPT provoke a stir? Quite simply, the CMPT made tourism official business. It wrote into law that the Mexican government not only endorsed tourism but also had chosen its starting lineup of representatives from related government ministries, the Bank of Mexico and other banking institutions, Chambers of Commerce and Industry, Hotel Associations, National Railways of Mexico, and other transportation companies. As a result, official and private tourist interests began to devise a development strategy that would enable Mexico to compete in the race for the tourist dollar. But first, they had to convince investors that this was a patriotic national industry and tourists that Mexico was indeed a safe holiday destination.

CHAPTER 2

STATE SUPPORT AND PRIVATE
INITIATIVE: PATTERNS IN THE
DEVELOPMENT AND PROMOTION
OF TOURISM, 1930–1935

In 1930, Editorial Mercurio, a publishing house in Mexico City managed by Francisco Borja Bolado[1] that was responsible for producing such magazines as *Social* and *MAPA*,[2] sent out a questionnaire about tourism to fellow Mexicans. It asked readers to return a one-page response to the following questions: "Do you think that recent events in Europe present Mexico with an opportunity to take immediate action to develop tourism on a grand scale? If so, what action should be taken?"[3] More than a public opinion poll, this questionnaire aimed to create a community of tourist supporters. As the Great Depression lay heavy on Mexico's economy and on those around the world, especially between the years 1931 and 1934, the momentum with which the state and private groups gained during the earliest promotion and development of tourism had almost entirely petered out. Unbeknown to tourist pioneers, especially Borja, it was not organizations, but individual tourist promoters—new and old, in Mexico and the United States—who kept the industry's wheels turning during these years of economic crisis.

In better economic circumstances, Mexico's tourist groups probably would have taken the next logical step. That is, they would have devised a strategy to develop tourist accommodations and services in preparation for the anticipated opening of the Nuevo Laredo-Mexico

City Highway in 1933.[4] In fact, organizations like the National Tourism Commission (CNT), Mexican American Automobile Association (AMAA), and others, had begun to outline development strategies. Even the Minister of Finance, Luis Montes de Oca, considered tax exemptions for those willing to invest capital in hotel construction.[5] But, by late 1930, the onset of economic depression foiled their earlier plans and exacerbated the national debt. What little funding the Finance Ministry promised the CNT for 1930, roughly Mex$200,000 pesos, they did not provide. The CNT's monthly meetings all but disappeared. To make matters worse, depleted government funds by 1932 delayed highway construction in Puebla, Taxco, and the Yucátan.[6] Proposals by U.S. publicity agents to begin promotional campaigns in favor of tourism to Mexico were rejected more than once by President Pascual Ortíz Rubio, who openly admitted that Mexico's government simply could not afford them. And, two years later, after several imploring letters from Consul Enrique D. Ruiz who repeatedly reported that the Ritz-Carlton Hotel chain and others were prepared to build deluxe hotels in Mexico City, the president replied frankly: "we are not sufficiently prepared to develop [them]."[7]

Although tourism's official voice—the federal government—failed to muster funds to develop needed infrastructure, tourists slowly but steadily trickled into Mexico even if they were perhaps no more comfortable than before. In fact, from 1930 to 1931 tourist entry nearly doubled from 24,000 to 41,000, and once the United States and Mexico finally showed signs of recovery in 1934, these same numbers increased fivefold.[8] Yet, transportation and communication were only slightly improved, and no new first-class hotel accommodations burst on the skyline in Mexico City. With what appeared to be an impoverished infrastructure, how did the tourist industry sustain these numbers? This chapter demonstrates that despite the government's inability to make much headway in tourist development, the steady numbers can be owed to the many private tourist entrepreneurs in Mexico and abroad who fomented the industry during these years.[9]

While economic depression crippled both government and even the emerging private tourist organizations, it made room for a growing number of supporters who rose to the occasion. These supporters, boosters if you will, many of whom were part of the Mexican revolutionary elite and others who were friends of Mexico, proposed to construct grand hotels (and some later did), lectured U.S. audiences about "the lure of Mexico," published laudatory articles about Mexico's tourism possibilities in U.S. newspapers, and updated Mexico's public about tourist news across the world. Proof of these efforts, sent directly to that Mexico's presidents and cabinet ministers, kept alive prospects for the industry. Moreover, unsolicited propaganda in favor of travel to Mexico published by friends in the United States helped ease fears among the general public about their supposed unruly and backward neighbor south of the border. Proposals for hotel construction drawn up by Mexican nationals kept the government interested, and articles in newspapers kept the public engaged in what would become, in just a few decades, one of Mexico's most successful national industries. In so doing, tourist boosters, in Mexico and the United States, not only expressed their support for this state-led industry but also proved their willingness to promote and fund tourism whether the government could or not.

EARLY GOVERNMENT EFFORTS TO DEVELOP TOURISM AND TO WIN SUPPORTERS

Before the Great Depression took the government's attention away from tourism, the official tourist organization, CNT, had begun to discuss plans for development. Members of the CNT had a basic understanding about how to build Mexico's tourist industry from earlier studies compiled by the Ministry of Foreign Affairs, from discussions held at meetings of previous tourist commissions and the AMAA, and from promotional efforts already carried out by the Bank of Mexico. They also received frequent reminders from the press, from tourist complaints, and from concerned persons who wrote letters to consuls emphasizing the need to build highways and hotels, to make entry through the border safe and easy for tourists, to provide tourist services like travel agencies and tour guides, and to produce publicity that would attract tourists to Mexico. Their comments, mostly in the form of criticism, focused particularly on inadequate tourist accommodations. For example, when a large excursion group of 750 railroad superintendents arrived in Mexico City in 1929, journalists reported that the city could only provide 700 individuals with decent accommodations. In response to this shameful lack of hotel rooms, one reporter wrote that like an infant, Mexican tourism might die in the crib. He concluded by asking the tourist commission why they bothered to organize when so little was being done to facilitate the construction of elegant, comfortable, large, and refined hotels.[10] Likewise, when the Nuevo Laredo-Monterrey section of Mexico's first international highway was ready for motorists, the press questioned its usefulness when no adequate accommodations for U.S. motorists existed along the highway or in Monterrey.[11]

Others reported on the grim problems found at Mexico's borders. Consuls reported that Americans believed it necessary to carry weapons to defend themselves against danger as they crossed the border, while others told of tourist complaints about abuses by local police, taxicab drivers, and businesses.[12] Another account encouraged the government to take measures to eradicate begging and vagrancy, especially in border towns where it was so prevalent because the image of poverty disagreed with tourists' objectives.[13] Tourists reported incidents of alleged incompetence on the part of border officials. Teddy Roosevelt's nephew, Theodore Douglas Robinson, was arrested on his train to Nogales for attempting to smuggle gold out of Mexico even though he had already declared it to officials and intended to exchange it. News of this incident spread throughout the U.S. press when customs officials detained him and his wife for the day and confiscated their gold.[14] In another incident, Philip Welhausen warned tourists about the Laredo Chamber of Commerce who cheated him by using an exchange rate well below the average.[15]

When members of the newly constituted National Tourism Commission organized the First National Tourist Conference held on April 20–27, 1930 at the Palace of Fine Arts, they took into account many of the previously made suggestions and criticisms. For the moment, issues related to development took precedence, while those related to border entry became secondary. Many believed the introduction of the so-called *tarjeta-pase* 11, or tourist card, had solved confusion and difficulties at the border. In preparation for the conference, organizers outlined four themes for presenters to address. First, the commission asked those interested in transportation and communication to focus on highways and railways as well as sea and airline routes. Second, members of the commission for accommodations and tourist comforts were required to discuss development plans for hotels in Mexico City, accommodations and restaurants along highways, and tourist services such as guides and travel agents. Third, those whose interests fell into the category of tourist attractions and safety were to present on Mexico's artistic beauty and archaeological ruins as well as the creation of new tourist attractions like beach resorts and spas. And, fourth, members of the commission for the coordination of general activities were to focus on methods to develop promotional campaigns, to create and organize local tourist committees, and to conserve the environment.[16] From the few conference papers available, it appears that members of local chambers of commerce, government officials at the national and local levels, and private entrepreneurs presented and discussed their visions for Mexico's future tourist industry. Taken together, these papers emphasized the need for private and local initiative for the industry's development. Eduardo de León, delegate from the Nuevo Laredo Chamber of Commerce and AMAA member, proposed that local financiers build a motel in Nuevo Laredo that provided tourists with basic accommodations and with entertainment for both adults and children. Such forms of entertainment included a cabaret, park, gym, and social club. He also proposed they build a "Foreign Club" to look like Chapultepec Castle, which would offer tourist accommodations like a dance hall, cantina, billiard room, gym, hair salon, and sports activities like tennis and basketball courts.[17] Alberto B. Girard gave a somewhat less lofty but more self-serving paper on his project to promote "The Touring Club of Mexico." As founder, Girard spoke about the benefits of a touring group modeled after the acclaimed Touring Club of France, whose purpose went well beyond promotion of motor travel alone. He argued that because the touring club would offer information on local hotels to members, it would no doubt boost hotel business. He also seconded Lucas de Palacio, at the time Mexico City's best-known hotelier, who suggested that bankers unite to form a National Hotel Credit Bank, and concluded his paper with the utmost patriotism when he stated that to be a member of the touring club was to be a good Mexican.[18]

Finally, Luis Montes de Oca enjoyed a heated debate with a delegate from the Local Tourist Committee of Veracruz, during a round-table discussion about improvements in port and border cities. Their confrontation began when Maraboto, the Veracruz representative, claimed that the local government must have misused federal funds because the inhabited area around the port lacked a drainage system and was in disrepair. Eduardo de León, from Monterrey, quickly pointed out that while Nuevo Laredo lacked electricity, water, and sanitation, the private sector had already begun to fund improvement projects. Montes de Oca asked Maraboto if the population was willing to pay for power and water. He then answered his own question: "You, Maraboto, have asked what the Federal Government will do to foment tourism in Veracruz? I tell you, nothing. It is an obligation of the port [and] of its inhabitants."[19]

Discussions about tourism that emerged from Mexico's first tourist conference highlighted the importance that private and local initiative would play in its future development. Above all, however, the greatest obstacle tourist pioneers faced was the lack of confidence in Mexico at home and abroad. Tourist pioneers were keenly aware of the poor impression that many Americans held about Mexico. Efforts to change negative impressions remained the highest priority for tourist promoters throughout these formative years before World War II when the Mexican and U.S. governments as well as Rockefeller's Office of Inter-American Affairs (OIAA) would help direct American tourists toward Latin America as a strategy to strengthen hemispheric solidarity.[20] But efforts to change American impressions of Mexico through the mass media and through an official tourist office in the United States were only halfheartedly employed by tourist groups in the late 1930s. Tourist developers had to find other ways to counter reports from the United States that told of the "fantastic dangers" in Mexico and reported on horrifying incidents like the female tourist who was mutilated in Jalisco by a band of robbers.[21] Because the Mexican government could not afford publicity campaigns in the United States, the tourist industry's success in the early 1930s relied on individuals to combat stories about Mexico as a dangerous neighbor.

Tourist promoters were also aware that Mexican investors by the early 1930s lacked confidence in the government's ability to foment industry and to stabilize the shaky political system. National identity was used by many to explain this failing. One prominent work by Samuel Ramos, *Profile of Man and Culture in Mexico*, argued that Mexicans suffered from an inferiority complex, the causes for which he found in early experiences of conquest and colonialism, and more recent tendencies toward imitations of European culture during the Porfiriato (1876–1911). As a result, Ramos argued that Mexicans wore masks that symbolized their fictitious personalities. He believed the remedy for this identity crisis to be self-knowledge and self-reflection, which would lead the nation toward a positive collective consciousness and a unified national identity.[22] Ramos's polemic points to the metamorphosis underway by the 1930s, but he overlooks more obvious catalysts for this supposed identity crisis. Namely, that some Mexicans, particularly those with capital, lacked confidence in their national economy. Efforts to develop tourism in part united the nation. It turned peoples' attention to the inherent customs that made Mexico unique and no doubt attractive to foreign tourists. The industry's success, then, relied on domestic support. Most importantly, it relied on Mexicans' investment of both labor and capital.

In the early years of the depression, Mexico's Finance Minister Luis Montes de Oca renewed talks with the International Bankers Committee to renegotiate the nation's loans, further crippling public confidence in Mexican industry both at home and abroad. This was readily admitted on one radio program in 1930 whose topic for the day was "Political Stability and the National Debt." The announcer explained that in addition to the present economic crisis, recent disorder and assaults had provoked doubts about his nation's political and economic stability.[23] Upon returning from meetings in New York, Luis Montes de Oca admitted to the nation that while the situation was grave, the public's optimism would help to ensure a better future.[24] In a speech to the National Bankers' Convention in 1931, he implored that its members work to regain the confidence of public opinion in an effort to combat the economic crisis.[25]

One strategy to renew confidence in the nation's economy was to build up public morale in industry. To do this, Mexico's government radio station XEN broadcast an hour-long program dedicated to reports on national industry and production. Organizers also arranged for the tour of "First Traveling Exhibit of National Products," designed to boost consumption of domestic goods and interest the public in new industries.[26] Among these industries, groups pitched tourism as the most natural and potentially profitable. Alberto B. Girard, founder of the Touring Club of Mexico, argued that tourism would become the most productive industry because, unlike mining or factory-line work, service laborers worked in the open air, on Acapulco beaches, in tranquil Taxco, near pyramids, and in cities. Girard argued that Mother Nature had given Mexico this potential industry, and support for it, which incidentally included membership into the Mexican Touring Club, was not only patriotic but also a way to demonstrate to the world how Mexico had advanced.[27]

The CNT also worked to win support for Mexico's tourist industry. In a series of essays in Spanish and English published in its first and only issue of *The National Tourist Magazine*, the government enticed readers in Mexico and the United States to support tourism. Essays not only highlighted its potential economic benefits for Mexico, but also its practical side as a medium for cultural understanding between nations.[28] The essays written for a U.S. audience worked to change negative impressions about Mexico by focusing on the state's campaign to ensure safe and modern travel. V. Mc. Dunn's piece invited Americans to take part in the new, working relationship between Mexico and the United States. Through travel, he argued, good will could replace ill will. He carefully emphasized that official groups in Mexico understood the importance of tourism and gave their support to the industry by building modern highways, airports, and accommodations, while railroad companies improved passenger service to Mexico.[29] Likewise, the president of Missouri Pacific Lines in Mexico, Colonel C.D. Hicks, geared his essay to individual tourists, not excursionists, who he believed held the key to Mexico's successful tourist industry. In this essay, he assured travel-minded Americans that as they searched for new recreational spots, prominent members of Mexico's official and private sectors were going to great lengths to make their nation the top tourist destination. For Mexico, he wrote, tourism offered a route toward progress that left dollars in the budget to expand agriculture, commerce, and manufacturing as well as to provide employment. In turn, for Americans, tourism to Mexico offered a route toward peace and understanding because they would find a hospitable and welcoming people.[30] Finally, R. J. Eustace, member of the Toledo Chamber of Commerce, related his impressions of Mexico while traveling through the country by automobile with representatives from the Bank of Mexico, National Railways of Mexico, and Mexican Railways. In this dramatic essay, he wrote that roads affected both Mexicans and Americans because they not only advanced the minds of people in rural communities through which the new roads passed, but also humanized "thousands of Americans who enter that country usually with fear, but who come out imbibed with the sincerity and beautiful mannerisms of a wonderful people."[31] Apparently, during his tour of Mexico, Eustace was profoundly affected by the many Mexicans in urban areas and remote villages who tossed fragrant flowers into his car. He concluded that tourists should expect to find a blend of European refinement, Asian exoticism and, above all, "music everywhere, music of pathos, music of Bagdad, music of Broadway."[32]

In an effort to alleviate fears of travel to Mexico, essays in the CNT's magazine played on Americans' sense of romanticism and national duty. But in its efforts to instill confidence in tourism as a lucrative industry, essays equally played on Mexicans' sense of national pride and their desire for modernity. Among the first images readers found was a full-page portrait of their President Pascual Ortíz Rubio espousing his views on tourism as progress, because, he argued, it required improved highways and railways that "mark the height of progress in a nation."[33] Like his colleagues, he believed that modern transportation civilized a nation, and tourism, he promised, promoted this end. Other feature stories echoed the president's sentiments. Members of the tourist commission from the Ministry of the Interior discussed the promise of tourism as a national industry. One official said that tourism both ensured progress and strengthened nationalism because the ability to attract foreign tourists brought with it a sense of respect for Mexico abroad. President of the CNT, Carlos Riva Palacio, emphasized tourism's potential role in economic growth but, more importantly, its role in transforming the minds of Mexican people.[34] Eduardo Vasconcelos wrote that tourism could help fulfill Mexico's aspirations: to strengthen the national economy, improve national solidarity (especially through the network of roads), and advance knowledge of national geography and history.[35] Another essay entitled, "Our Goals," explained that while the tourist deserved Mexico's respect because their money helped the economy by taking nothing away, Mexicans in turn deserved respect from tourists.[36] Finally, Felix Palavicini reassured the public that members of the CNT and other tourist groups were not only patriotic, but also business leaders who know that, with little investment, tourism would become the greatest national business.[37] By linking tourist development to the nationalist cause, revolutionary elites hoped to bolster support for this industry.

Another prominent tourist organization that emerged in 1929 echoed the CNT's efforts. Whereas the Bank of Mexico's Department of Tourism disappeared in 1932 when its mastermind Albert Mascareñas resigned as director, the Mexican Automobile Association (AMA), formerly the AMAA, remained a prominent, if financially weak, force in promoting motor tourism during these depression years, especially in Monterrey and along the U.S.-Mexico border.[38] Like the federal government, they faced a grave problem: how to finance their labors. Through membership they found resources to provide services to tourists and to promote Mexico in the United States. The AMA became outspoken about motor travel to and within Mexico by the mid- to late 1930s. In August 1932, AMA officials opened an Office of Information in Nuevo Laredo where they distributed maps and their English-language monthly magazine *Monterrey Greeter*, which provided a guide to local attractions. In a bold move, they sponsored a tour of Monterrey for U.S. journalists, paid the cost of room and board, and in return, received flattering write-ups about motoring to Monterrey, a tactic later repeated by other tourist groups by the late 1930s. Other publicity events employed by the AMA was a car race from Laredo to Monterrey to introduce American drivers to the newly paved, just completed Nuevo Laredo-Monterrey section of the international highway that was expected to be completed by 1933, but delayed until 1936 due to financial problems. During the Great Depression, they also produced a pamphlet entitled, "Monterrey All the Year Round" and a brochure of images from Mexico City to be distributed at the Chicago World's Fair. Despite the AMA's continued efforts, financial crisis retarded the fulfillment of their goals. By late 1933, more than half its members failed to pay yearly dues, and the CNT, placed briefly under the wings of the Ministry of National Economy, did not hurry to assist their publicity campaign in the United States. In its own words, the AMA could not develop tourism to its fullest potential.[39]

Certainly, these early efforts by members of the AMA played a role in sustaining the modest numbers of tourists entering Mexico during the Great Depression but they were not alone. In addition to Mexico's government, friends from the North who helped make Mexican culture and art fashionable in the U.S. popular imagination during the 1920s also threw their support behind tourism. Boosters included scholars of Mexico and businessmen who longed to see their neighbor advance and their wallets engorge. Together with Mexico's revolutionary elite these tourist boosters helped promote the industry during the early 1930s. While they made little headway in terms of development and profit, their cooperation reflected the broad network and breadth of Mexico's team of supporters who in no small way helped their neighbor prepare for entry into the competition for the tourist dollar.

AMERICAN TOURIST PROMOTERS

By the late 1920s, cultural relations between the United States and Mexico had improved with the help of U.S. artists, intellectuals, and journalists. As Helen Delpar has shown, art promoters like Alma Reed and Frances Flynn Paine organized major exhibits in New York City, the most successful of which was Diego Rivera's one-man show at the Museum of Modern Art in 1932 sponsored by Paine's Mexican Art Association. Through other media such as music and scholarship, Americans heard the talent of Carlos Chávez, Mexico's greatest composer,[40] and university students read works by Frank Tannenbaum while others signed up for Hubert Herring's educational tours of Mexico.[41] Architects also mediated these cultural exchanges when Francisco R. Mariscal accepted an invitation by The Architectural League of New York to organize an exhibit on Mexico in 1931.[42] While these political and cultural pilgrims succeeded in reshaping prevailing views of "barbarous" Mexico, their efforts reached only a small sector of the broader American traveling audience. In particular, they shaped the growing excursionist movement in which students, academics, and philanthropists visited for the purpose of exchanging knowledge or of acquiring art. For example, Mr. and Mrs. Rockefeller toured Mexico City with Frances Flynn Paine in 1933 to buy folk art and to meet fellow philanthropist and former finance minister, Luis Montes de Oca.[43] Still, the success of Mexico's tourist industry depended on what one journalist referred to as the true, sensual tourist who visited Mexico not as an intellectual, a businessperson, or an artist but as a tourist in search of a place to spend his or her holiday. This average American tourist, he argued, came for recreation: to see bullfights, folkloric dances, exotic Indians, and to get to know its customs for the mere thrill of travel to a foreign land.[44] This tourist who represented middle-class America formed an audience for whom cultural and political pilgrims could not so easily convince of Mexico's worth as a tourist destination.

Early on, tourist supporters found that the average American remained skeptical despite the work carried out by these pilgrims and despite the official word from Mexico's government that they were dedicated to fomenting tourism and to ensuring tourists' safety. One railroad promoter pointed out to a government official in 1929 that the overwhelming feeling about Mexico in the United States was pessimistic.[45] American impressions of Mexico were so bleak that Alexandria, Louisiana mayor, V.V. Lamkin, urged President Portes Gil to send government officials dressed in military and police uniforms on a tour throughout the United States to impress upon potential tourists the idea that Mexico was a safe destination for holidaymaking. He wrote that this would be effective because "people here think that should they go to Mexico and do the least offense, they will be immediately put in jail and held for ransom."[46]

To change popular opinion and to reach a wider audience, friends of Mexico and U.S. business interests gave speeches and published articles that described the recent changes that had taken place in that Mexico. Their goal was to reassure the typical tourist that travel was safe, easy, and valuable. In 1928, Robert J. Eustace of the Toledo, Ohio Chamber of Commerce delivered a series of lectures on Mexico that praised the federal government's recent accomplishments and the nation's natural beauty.[47] Likewise, in 1929 Dr. Lincoln Wirt gave a speech at the San Francisco Commonwealth Club entitled, "The Lure of Mexico," in which he related his experience as a member of Professor Herring's Seminar on Cultural Relations with Latin America, an experience that changed his own impression of Mexico formerly based on images of seedy border towns. Instead, he told the audience that he found a capital city as beautiful and modern as any in Europe. Apparently, his experience taking in an opera at the Palace of Fine Arts proved that Mexican people were respectable when the actors did not kiss, did not bare their legs, did not kick high, and did not smoke, which left a "clean taste in the mouth."[48] Finally, directors of the Houston radio station KPRC dedicated a musical concert to the Mexican people in 1929 by playing traditional Mexican ballads for their local listeners designed to represent well things Mexican to a broader audience.[49]

American journalists, many of whom visited Mexico for the first time in the early 1930s, published articles and proposed publicity campaigns to combat the overwhelming negative view of their southern neighbor. Just one month after President Ortíz Rubio safely escaped an attempted assassination on his life, Cornelius Vanderbilt Jr. published his interview with the president in New York City's *American*. During the interview, Vanderbilt asked the president to outline his tourist plan. The president did so by emphasizing the sense of safety U.S. tourists would experience upon their arrival and mentioned development plans to build modern hotels in Mexico City. Another journalist from the *Los Angeles Times* praised rapid travel to Mexico on the Pullman railroad service between Mexico City and St. Louis, and the new air service between Texas, California, and Mexico City.[50] And, Leslie W. Tuttle, ticket agent for Northern Pacific Railway Company and amateur journalist, published a five-part series on Mexico in the *Tacoma News Tribune*. In one article entitled "Mexico Stable and Fast Making Progress," Tuttle told readers about improved economic and political conditions as well as advances in transportation and hotel construction.[51]

In addition, boosters also worked to attract Americans by publishing tour guides and maps. One of the most active was Wagons Lits-Cook Travel Agency that opened an office at the invitation of the National Bank of Mexico and worked under the leadership of Oreste Cabutti in Mexico City. In 1932, Wagons Lits published an English-language travel brochure, "How to See Mexico and its Surroundings," with a special emphasis on day trips from Mexico City. Excursion prices ranged from Mex$11 to Mex$15, took tourists through Mexico City, to Puebla and Cholula, to Tepotzlán and the Desert of the Lions, to Teotihuacán pyramids, to Xochimilco, and to Cuernavaca. Tourists also enjoyed lectures about the sights and lunch. The brochure likely had wide distribution in the United States because it was sent out to Mexican consulates for dissemination.[52] Missouri Pacific Railways was also active in publishing promotional literature when in 1931 they distributed books with photographs of Mexico, provoking both delight and frustration—delight because the images were beautiful and frustration because the company had already received complaints by tourists that Mexico City, and Mexico in general, could not provide adequate accommodations to visitors. This, the president admitted, was both fair and true.[53]

Other friends of Mexico and U.S. business interests tried to strike deals with the Mexican government in promote tourism in Mexico. After his first visit to Mexico with a group of California journalists in 1930, M.F. Hoyl wrote to President Ortíz Rubio that his trip was a revelation of sorts in which he replaced his delusions about a wild, semicivilized nation with admiration for its natural beauty and optimism for its future. He suggested that through a good press agent (of course alluding to himself), the dissemination of negative propaganda in the United States would end and thousands of tourists would flood Mexico.[54] One *New York Times* journalist even traveled to Mexico to meet with the president's secretary at which time he proposed to direct a promotional campaign in the U.S. press. At a mere US$65,000 per year, he offered Mexico's government an opportunity to create and strengthen confidence among U.S. readers in Mexico as a politically and economically stable nation. Unfortunately, Mexico's president twice refused his offer because he lacked federal funds.[55] In 1932, Dr. Joseph Eller (former president Calles's son-in-law) met with representatives from U.S. transportation and finance companies—Pan American Airways, Eastern Airport Service, J.P. Morgan, Harriman Bank & Trust Co., and Penn Railroad—in an effort to raise capital to open a tourist agency in Mexico City. And, two members of the Ciudad Juárez Chamber of Commerce asked the government to pressure the National Railways of Mexico to lower their prices from Texas to Mexico City so that they might offer discount excursions to the capital.[56] The manager of Latino American Films pitched the idea to the Interior Ministry that his company produce films to promote tourism.[57] Others in search of official support for their tourist promotion projects appealed directly to the president. For example, José J. Razo asked President Ortíz Rubio to help him establish the Mexican Tourist Company, a company responsible for producing and distributing promotional literature, and for financing the construction of hotels and tourist training schools. Professor Campo N. Bolaños asked the president to be an honorary member of his proposed Mexican Financing Society that sought to raise capital for the extension of tourist services along Mexico's highways.[58]

TOURIST DEVELOPMENT

Efforts by tourist boosters in the United States and Mexico between the years 1930 and 1934 helped sustain interest in the industry's potential. During these years, individuals without financial support from the Mexican government took the initiative to change unflattering impressions of Mexico in the United States, and proposed ways to increase tourist traffic. While many of their plans never materialized, it was only a matter of time before other projects like hotel construction reached fruition. Fortunately for the government, tourist pioneers had been working since 1930 to shore up ties with U.S. hotel companies and with domestic investors. However, as chapter 3 points out, because of economic nationalism, the revolutionary elite in the mid- to late 1930s tried their best to keep American capital, but not American know-how, out of the tourist industry, and to place it instead in the hands of Mexican nationals. The rush to build hotels, especially in the capital city, was almost entirely choreographed by prominent Mexican individuals and corporations. Nevertheless, future hoteliers took many of their cues from those in the United States, as the 1938 dinner between American hoteliers and Mexican elites suggests.

Enrique D. Ruiz, Mexican consul in New York, best illustrates the kind of tourist advocate who sought to forge early relations with prominent American business interests. At his post for several years, Ruiz became friendly with Luis Montes de Oca, who frequently sought solace with his nieces in New York after two important resignations as minister of finance and as director of the Bank of Mexico. Ruiz had also developed good relations with members of the Mexican Chamber of Commerce in New York. By 1929, he took an avid interest in fomenting U.S. tourism to Mexico, especially in hotel construction in the capital city. For Ruiz, tourism meant progress for Mexico and its success relied on providing tourists with deluxe accommodations. No doubt, his experience in cosmopolitan New York City shaped his desire to seek investment from some of the most prominent U.S. hotel companies. He arranged a tentative agreement with Ritz-Carlton Hotels in 1930 after meeting its president, George McAneny, who assured Ruiz that his company would construct a hotel of grand style in the capital using American know-how and investors from both sides of the border.[59] Unfortunately, Ruiz never finalized the deal with Ritz-Carlton, and his frustration with the slow development of the tourist industry grew over the years. In one angry letter to the new president, Jorge U. Orozco, Ruiz impressed upon government officials the urgency to build deluxe hotels in Mexico City. This time he received a dreadful response from his personal the president's secretary stating that Mexico was in no financial position to develop them.[60]

Likewise, Jorge M. Orozco, another Mexican living in New York City, acted as the intermediary between U.S. and Mexican interests.

A friend of Luis Montes de Oca and the president, Orozco wrote letters to them on behalf of Dr. O. Friedlieb, an American businessman interested in building a resort in northern Baja California. Friedlieb proposed to turn 4,539 hectares of land from the San Antonio de los Buenos de Mendoza Ranch into a resort like those found along the French and Italian Riviera. He planned to provide tourists with luxurious accommodations, exquisite food, beach recreation, and a club-casino.[61] In his letter to the president, Orozco recalled his old friendship with then-president Pascual Ortíz Rubio in hopes that he would give Friedlieb's proposal the support that it required.[62]

In addition to the role Mexicans in the United States played in forging relationships with American investors, the National Railways of Mexico commissioned studies of hotel life as a way to pinpoint the nation's most urgent need to increase tourist traffic. In 1930, both the National Railways of Mexico and the Missouri Pacific Railway Company of Mexico asked Frank A. Dudley, president of the United States Hotels Company of America, to examine hotels in Mexico and to outline the best plan for establishing a chain of first-class hotels. He reported in 1930 that the only hotel he considered first class, and thus satisfactory for American tourists, was the Hotel Geneve, owned and operated by Tómas S. Gore.[63] Nevertheless, Dudley reported that its restaurants, lobby, and kitchen were in urgent need of renovation. In 1931, Gore made these renovations by adding 180 rooms to the original 120 and by installing a private bath in all the rooms.[64] In his report, Dudley argued that hotels in Mexico, particularly in Mexico City, not only lacked appeal for the well-to-do American tourist, but also failed to appeal to even the middle class. This, he wrote, proved the greatest obstacle for transportation companies whose trains were nearly empty. Dudley repeated these conclusions in meetings with the president and with the minister of finance in which he suggested that a company modeled after his own, the United Hotels Company of Mexico, be created with capital from the Mexican government, transportation companies, and his company. He also suggested that a modern, high-class hotel geared to satisfy American tourists' needs be constructed in Mexico City to reflect traditional Mexican and Spanish architecture and that it be built away from the *Zócalo* (central plaza). Finally, he suggested that Mexicans build smaller hotels in places like San Luis Potosí, Guadalajara, Mazatlán, and Guaymas.[65] While tourist developers did not team up with Dudley to realize his building projects, many of his suggestions became a part of Mexico's project of hotel construction.

One hotel group, the Companía Explotadora de Hoteles, S.A., formed in 1932 by three Mexicans, proposed the first of many projects to build deluxe hotels with domestic capital and with assistance from the private sector. The life of their project on paper is as interesting as the hotel whose name began as Palace Hotel but changed to Hotel del Prado by the mid-1940s and was located on Avenida Juárez at Revillagigedo. In 1932, Alonso Peón (a Mexican living in the United States), Adolfo Prieto, and Agustín Legorreta (director of the National Bank of Mexico) commissioned prominent architect, Carlos Obregón Santacilia, to draw up plans for the Hotel Palace to be constructed on the lot of the ex-Hospicio de Pobres near the Alameda Central. The basis for the proposal, seconded by both the President Abelardo L. Rodríguez and Finance Minister Alberto J. Pani, was the immediate need for a first-class hotel in Mexico City in anticipation of the completed Nuevo Laredo-Mexico City Highway. This proposal also fulfilled what Pani described in his memoir as the "Calles Plan," which included widespread modernization projects like road construction and tourist development. Their hotel required official approval because part of the lot was government property, the ex-Hospicio and the fire station. Both Pani and Rodríguez responded favorably to their proposal and recognized their plan as a service to the nation.[66]

Yet, the Compañía Explotadora faced the same lack of capital as other tourist developers during these years. By 1933, they approached the National Railways of Mexico for an investment of an additional Mex$1 million, the El Aguila oil company for Mex$40,000 and the Compañía Fundadora de Fierro y Acero de Monterrey for Mex$260,000. As a result, National Railways embarked on another study of hotel life in and tourist entry to Mexico City in an effort to measure the viability of the "Hotel Palace" project. The partners planned to construct an eight-story hotel with 500 rooms. All the rooms would be equipped with private bathrooms and telephones, and ten suites would have an added office space. On the street level they planned to build ten offices for rent, hair salons, a cantina, grill room, lonchería (casual, diner-style restaurant) as well as the main, passenger, and automobile entrances. On the main floor they planned for a lobby, fine restaurant, movie house, beauty salon, seven retail stores, tourism and travel agencies, and eight locales for services such as a tobacco store and pharmacy. Finally, the mezzanine would house a ballroom for parties, a banquet hall, private dining rooms, and general hotel offices. Most appealing to government officials was that the project would provide nearly 150 new jobs including hotel managerial staff, bellboys, maids, and maintenance workers. The proposal indicated that National Railways and other potential investors stood to earn an estimated Mex$2 million each month.[67]

The saga of the Palace Hotel and the Compañía Explotadora is murky. Some evidence bears out that by 1935, National Railways President Luis Cabrera suggested that the Palace Hotel be no less luxurious, but smaller in size. The statistics on tourist traffic showed that while Americans increasingly entered Mexico only about 34,000 tourists—individuals and excursionist groups—reached Mexico City. This suggested that there was no real need to build a hotel with 500 or more rooms.[68] Nonetheless, no evidence has been found on the completed Palace Hotel. Instead, by late 1930, the Palace Hotel went bankrupt and the federal government took the shares formerly held by its three original founders and commissioned its original architect, Obregón Santacilia, to draw up plans for what became the Hotel del Prado, which opened in 1948.

Still, the Palace Hotel first imagined in 1932 by a group of Mexican investors illustrates broader factors at play in the development of the tourist industry. In many ways, it laid the groundwork for future hotel construction at least until the mid-1940s. The push to construct a grandiose hotel in Mexico City just as the expected Nuevo Laredo-Mexico City Highway was complete foreshadowed what became a boom in hotel construction by 1936 when the highway finally opened to motorists. Tourist advocates and organizations refocused their energies on motor travel specifically, and on promoting and developing Mexico City as the center for all tourist activity. As a result, the capital emerged as the hub for the tourist industry. Finally, the history of the Palace Hotel hints at the future politics of tourist development, namely that investment was rooted largely in Mexico and reflected a conglomeration of interested individuals and private groups all closely linked to tourism, including oil and railway companies as well as former presidents and finance ministers. Ironically, when Finance Minister Alberto J. Pani resigned from his post and from more than 20 years of public service, he turned to the most natural investment venture, hotel construction. In just three years, Pani and investors who made up Edificios Modernos, S.A. built one of Mexico City's finest hotels, Hotel Reforma, which was eventually sold to an American company in 1952.[69]

*   *   *

Expressions of support for tourism from the Compañía Explotadora and those discussed in this chapter—journalists, private businesses, and others—were heard during the industry's early years, especially as the depression weakened those initial efforts from early tourist organizations. These advocates set a pattern of cooperation between private and government associations for others to follow. Rather than allow this potentially profitable industry to wither away during the economic depression, individual boosters kept Mexico geared up to compete in the race for the tourist dollar that was just on the horizon. As the revolutionary elite fortified working relationships between Mexico and the United States, and between individuals and companies in Mexico, they garnered support for tourist development by emphasizing the nationalist sentiment inherent in this industry that brought about economic development and a modern infrastructure. With galvanized support at home and abroad, Mexico's tourist developers began to promote their nation as a product to the American consumer.

CHAPTER 3

MOTORING TO MEXICO: HIGHWAYS, HOTELS, AND *LO MEXICANO*, 1936–1938

Mexico's National Road Commission organized the inauguration of the Nuevo Laredo-Mexico City Highway[1] to take place on July 1, 1936 after eight years of construction (1928–1936) and a total investment of Mex$62 million. In a four-day ceremony that commenced on the International Bridge uniting Laredo, Texas with Nuevo Laredo, Tamaulipas, Mexican and U.S. delegates representing the Mexican Automobile Association (AMA), the American Automobile Association (AAA), and the Ministry of Communications and Public Works (SCOP) began an inaugural motor tour of the highway. Delegates toured Monterrey, stayed the evening at the Hotel Mante in Villa Juárez, San Luis Potosí and in Zimapán, Hidalgo, and stopped for lunch in Pachuca, Hidalgo as they made their way toward Mexico City where festivities organized by the municipal government and the American Colony awaited them. On July 4, the American delegation returned to Nuevo Laredo by special train.[2] The official opening of the Nuevo Laredo-Mexico City Highway was monumental. The highway functioned metaphorically as a bridge between previously fractured nations and created a sense of Panamericanism and "good neighborliness," two ideas ingrained in promotional campaigns for tourism after 1936. More literally, it became Mexico's principal artery to which future roads within Mexico would connect. The opening ushered in a new developmental phase in the evolution of Mexico's tourist industry. Official and private groups expected a threefold increase in tourist entries to Mexico. And, they were right: between the years 1935 and 1937 the number of American motor tourists entering Mexico through Nuevo Laredo increased more than 50 percent, from 14,500 to 29,000.[3] In fact, this increase in numbers mirrored broader changes in automobile ownership in the United States where the number of private automobile registrations from 1920 to 1930 increased from 1 car per 13 people to 1 car per 5 people; by 1940, the U.S. Department of Transportation had on record more than 27 million private automobile registrations.[4] Indeed motor travel, and especially motor travel for pleasure, contributed to broader concepts of democracy and freedom inherent in American national identity by the early to mid-twentieth century.[5] To attract and to satisfy this growing market, government and private enterprise faced the urgent need to develop services and accommodations as well as to beautify Mexico's border towns and its capital city.

The Mexican Automobile Association (AMA), a group with extensive experience, worked quickly to meet the demand for hotels, motels, and restaurants along the highway and to provide tourist services on the border and in Mexico City. With only a few hundred members and two offices in Monterrey and Mexico City in 1935, the AMA only one year later expanded its network throughout the republic and across the border just as the highway opened. By 1938, they had successfully convinced Mexican elites to invest or to loan capital for the completion of highways, hotels, and motels and they forged relationships with important groups in the United States, including the American Automobile Association. They even hired four U.S. representatives stationed in San Antonio, New Orleans, Washington, DC, and St. Louis to promote the idea of motor travel to Mexico. One of these representatives in San Antonio, William Furlong, a longtime friend of Mexico, toured the United States to promote the new Nuevo Laredo-Mexico City Highway and even published a monthly newsletter, "The Furlong Service," which reported on Mexico's road conditions for American motor tourists. By the time Luis Montes de Oca, the former finance minister, director of the Bank of Mexico, and president of the AMA, founded the Mexican Tourist Association in 1939 the AMA had already transformed Mexico's tourist industry.

Nevertheless, no single private or official organization operated alone to build Mexico's tourist industry. Instead, the Automobile Association cooperated with members from a new group, the National Tourism Committee (CTNT), formed by the government in response to the opening of the Nuevo Laredo-Mexico City Highway. This organization reflected the government's continuing effort to mobilize private enterprise. As a subsidiary of the government's Department of Tourism, then under the direction of the Interior Ministry, members of the CTNT included invited representatives from major transportation and oil companies, banking institutions, travel agencies, and hotels, many who also belonged to the AMA. Even the AMA sent a delegate to the CTNT. In contrast to its predecessors—the Mixed Pro-Tourism Commission, formed by the government in 1929, and the National Tourism Commission, formed by the government in 1930—the CTNT was prolific in promoting tourism, especially after 1938.

The AMA and the CTNT owed their success in part to the relative peace and stability enjoyed throughout Mexico during the presidency of Lázaro Cárdenas (1934–1940), especially after he exiled Plutarco Elías Calles in 1935. Scholars have traditionally characterized Cárdenas as the personification of the revolution, renowned for his nationalization of oil and his redistribution of communal landholdings[6] and have only recently come to recognize him for his pro-industrial, pro-capitalist agenda, in this case tourist development.[7] By the end of his six-year term, as war raged in Europe, he earmarked what amounted to US$10,000 in government funds to the Mexican Tourist Association for a one-month publicity campaign in the United States. Ultimately, organizations like the AMA and CTNT owed their success to their own members, who formed an ever-expanding constellation of elite players from the government to private business in Mexico, especially Mexico City, and in the United States. Enrique Krauze has argued that the state expanded its economic role by the late 1920s because "Mexico had no social class that could, through its own efforts, draw the country toward material progress."[8] Certainly those involved in the development and promotion of the tourist industry, especially AMA members, represented a new social class that emerged by 1936 more capable than the government to push Mexico toward prosperity.[9] In so doing, Mexico became a premier holiday destination at the close of World War II.

DEVELOPING TOURIST ACCOMMODATIONS AND SERVICES: THE AMA

Six months before the opening of the Nuevo Laredo-Mexico City Highway, Mexican delegates attended the annual convention of the American Road Builders Association (ARBA) held in Cleveland, Ohio. Participants reported that many of the nearly 10,000 participants, most from the United States and Canada, expressed interest in

Mexico's highways and eagerness for the opening of the new international highway. The Mexican government also sent an official representative from the Department of Tourism, Ignacio L. Hijar, who gave a series of lectures to sell Mexico as a tourist destination. Moreover, representatives from the Ministry of Communications and Public Works (SCOP), National Railways, AMA, and the Department of Tourism set up an exhibit at the convention. Two Mexican women dressed as the typical *china poblana* staffed the booth and male delegates to the conference wore typical *charro* attire.[10] William Furlong, secretary of the Inter-American Highway Association, helped by showing films about the soon-to-open Nuevo Laredo-Mexico City Highway.[11]

At the Pan-American session of the conference, Hijar gave an inspiring speech about the state of tourism in Mexico. He spoke about President Cárdenas's programs to complete highways and build hotels, and formally invited the entire audience to visit the "land of wonders."[12] Nevertheless, in reports to the Department of Tourism following the conference he bitterly echoed what others before him had pointed out—that Mexico lacked tourist services and accommodations, had anachronistic and unsanitary border towns, and offered few diversions in the capital.[13] Hijar was so dismayed by the slow development of tourist infrastructure that he even suggested that they postpone the highway inauguration until these problems were resolved.

Just seven years earlier, on the way back to Mexico after the 1929 ARBA conference, Mexican delegates threw their support behind tourist development after they stopped in San Antonio to form an association whose name later became the Mexican Automobile Association (AMA). Its parent organization sought to foment motor tourism in northern Mexico, especially Monterrey, to foster membership in its Monterrey and Mexico City clubs and to develop the infrastructure and services necessary to build a tourist industry just when the Nuevo Laredo-Monterrey section of the larger international highway opened.[14] Like motor clubs in Europe and the United States, the AMA promoted automobile driving in Mexico by offering services to its members and to tourists. In 1933, with 205 members, the AMA opened an Office of Information and Finance in Nuevo Laredo where they distributed tourist literature and maps, exchanged currency, offered automobile insurance and temporary memberships. They also held their second road race from Laredo to Monterrey in an effort to publicize the newly paved highway. In the same year, they continued to produce pamphlets on Monterrey and brochures on Mexico City, and to pressure SCOP to complete highway construction and the Department of Tourism, then under the Ministry of National Economy, to develop publicity for dissemination in the United States.[15] Before 1934, the AMA had difficulty garnering members and funds. The worldwide economic crisis retarded its growth and the development of Mexico's tourist industry in general. But by 1938 the association grew to more than 4,000 members in its Mexico City branch alone—up from 205 members in both offices only 5 years earlier.[16] With such a membership, board members decided to open four additional clubs in Puebla, Guadalajara, Mazatlán, and Torreón, and to organize eight new delegations in Nuevo Laredo, Ciudad Mante, Ciudad Valles, Linares, Pachuca, Toluca, Orizaba, and Mérida. Finally, it opened four honorary groups in San Antonio at the St. Anthony Hotel, in New Orleans at the Whitney Building, in Washington, DC at the National Press Building, and in St. Louis at the Hart Building. William Furlong in San Antonio and Andres Horcasitas in New Orleans included some of its American representatives.

AMA members increasingly reflected the most prominent sectors of Mexican society, including the revolutionary elite who fought in the revolution and served as revolutionary presidents and ministers, and friends from the American Colony. These revolutionaries turned businessmen got down from their horses and got into a Cadillac by using their connections in official and private sectors to develop the tourist infrastructure so desperately needed by 1936.[17] For more than two decades, the Mexican Automobile Association flourished under the leadership of Luis Montes de Oca. Born in Mexico City in 1894, Montes de Oca enjoyed an illustrious career in government and in banking. A certified public accountant, he served as Venustiano Carranza's civilian aide during the revolution. He held the position as consul general of Mexico in El Paso, Hamburg, and Paris, and served on the presidential cabinet as finance minister from 1927 until 1932 when he resigned once his plan to shift the economy from gold to cash currency floundered and General Calles withdrew his support. He lived for some time in New York City where he frequently met with old friends who ran J.P. Morgan Co. like Chairman Thomas Lamont and friends of Mexico like Frances Paine, renowned for organizing art exhibits of prominent Mexican painters like Diego Rivera and for her connections with philanthropists like the Rockefellers. In 1934, he returned to Mexico to begin his term as director of the Bank of Mexico between the years 1935 and 1940.

A true nationalist, Montes de Oca dedicated himself to promoting a cultured and beautiful Mexico City. He lived in San Ángel and eventually built a second home in Cuernavaca, the most fashionable

place to live in the 1920s–1930s.[18] He was an avid gardener and tree
lover who ordered rare plants and flowers almost monthly from
American suppliers. He worked with Miguel Ángel de Quevedo to
preserve the natural environment of Mexico City and to build gardens
and parks. In 1938, he even hired two forestry experts from Davey
Tree Expert Company in Kent, Ohio to drive a trailer filled with equip-
ment to Mexico City in order to save the life of trees at Chapultepec
Sports Club.[19] He sat as a board member on the Mexico City
Planning Commission and had been involved in urban planning meetings as early as 1930. As a patron of the arts, he served as a longtime
board member of the Mexico Symphony Orchestra and lent his
financial expertise as its treasurer in the 1930s.

Montes de Oca dedicated much of his career to serving the
revolutionary government. As director of the Bank of Mexico under
Cárdenas, Montes de Oca doubled as president of the Mexican
Banker's Association and was most active in establishing lending insti-
tutions. He founded the Asociación Hipotecaria Mexicana (Mexican
Mortgage Association) in 1936 and the Banco de Crédito Hotelero
(Hotel Credit Bank) in 1937. These institutions helped finance hotel
construction across the republic, especially in Acapulco, Mexico City,
and along the new international highway. Companies like Campos
Mexicanos de Turismo, S.A., founded by former president Pascual
Ortíz Rubio with capital from members of the Mexico City Chamber
of Commerce, applied more than once to the Mortgage Association
for loans to complete motel construction in Ciudad Valles, San Luis
Potosí, a common rest stop along the new highway.[20] As finance minister when the government first declared its intent to develop tourism
in Mexico, Montes de Oca spoke publicly about the prospects of
tourism as the ideal national industry. He argued that tourism would
not only modernize Mexico, but would also serve as a source of great
profits for the government and for private business. Tourism encom-
passed many of Montes de Oca's interests, and through the AMA he
dedicated more than two decades to its development. He specially
ordered the latest books on tourism and hotel management in Spanish,
English, French, and Italian.[21] He also promoted motor travel as the
latest leisure activity, sporting his own collection of automobiles,
including Cadillac's latest models.

Through the AMA, Montes de Oca organized motor parades to
promote automobile purchases and national tourism on the nation's
new highways. In 1937, for example, on the north side of the Alameda,
the AMA, automobile dealers, and the Mexico City Transit Office
organized a festival on safe driving that included a parade of transit

officers, the Red Cross, firemen, and, of course, new car models for 1937. Representatives and their wives from the city's automobile dealerships participated in the parade by driving two new cars in a procession. Their wives advertised the dealership and car brand on a sash worn across their chest.[22]

Montes de Oca revolutionized Mexico's tourist industry through the AMA, banking institutions and, later, the Mexican Tourist Association. But, he did not act alone. Additional AMA founding members, José Rivera R., employee of the National Road Commission, and Antonio L. Rodríguez, employee of the Bank of Mexico who pioneered tourism in Monterrey in 1929, also dedicated their careers toward developing it. The association's board members included president of the "Azteca" Insurance Company, Cayetano Blanco Vigil, whose insurance policies were sold to AMA members; Tómas Gore, owner of the Hotel Geneve; honorary board member Ing. Vicente Cortes Herrera, president of the National Highway Commission, director of Colonial Buildings and Monuments (preservation department in the National Institute of Arts and History), sub-secretary of SCOP, and the first director of the newly created Petróleos Mexicanos (Pemex) after oil nationalization in 1938; and Aarón Sáenz Garza, sub-secretary of the Ministry of Foreign Affairs, former governor of Nuevo León, head of the Mexico City government, cofounder of Mexicana Airlines and president of the Banco Azúcarero.

Whereas these men, particularly Montes de Oca, Sáenz, and Herrera, bridged the gap between private business and government, members of the AMA-Mexico City Club constituted the capital city's most prominent figures from the private sector. In July 1936, the AMA created a committee to study and make recommendations for local tourist services in preparation for the increase in U.S. motorists. They invited prominent transportation interests such as Amos R. Coleman, manager of the Department of Tourism of the Pierce Oil Company, W.P. Flower, manager of Huasteca Petroleum Company, P. Williams, manager of "El Aguila" Oil Company, F.C. Mack, manager of the California S. Oil Company, and Leonicio Pazzi, manager of the Hotel Regis.[23] By 1938, AMA-Mexico City board members included the most prominent revolutionary elite such as Francisco Lona, manager of National Railways of Mexico (FFCCN), Luis Osio y Torres Rivas, president of the National Chamber of Hotels, Lucas de Palacio, president of the Mexican Hotel Association (AMH), and Pedro Gorozpe, manager of the Hotel Ritz.[24]

With members such as those just described, it is no surprise then that the AMA was successful at fulfilling its goals to promote motor tourism and to develop tourist services and accommodations. Just as the Nuevo Laredo-Mexico City Highway opened to motorists in 1936, José Rivera R. began to organize AMA-affiliated delegations in major towns and cities along the highway in an effort to ensure the existence of tourist facilities and to inspire local groups to develop tourist accommodations. The AMA also began to compile data on hotels, restaurants, gas stations, and car repair services for promotional literature that they distributed to tourists as they entered through Nuevo Laredo. When Rivera began his tour along the new highway in July, he found that Ciudad Valles was the only location in which motorists would find more than one or two hotels; in fact, the city had five hotels.[25] By August, Rivera reported that he succeeded in organizing delegations in Nuevo Laredo, Ciudad Valles, and Pachuca.

Despite the overwhelming opinion in the communities that these towns offered little to the tourist and the tourist offered little to these towns, Rivera managed to convince prominent community members to form affiliated groups. Members worked in sectors of commerce and industry that related to tourism. Part of the Nuevo Laredo delegation, for example, included David Marcial who worked for the Bank of Mexico in Nuevo Laredo, Customs Agent Robert Zuñiga, Juan Rendón who owned Hotel Rendón, Fidencio Rendón and Vicente Peña who owned automobile dealerships, and Oscar Caso who ran a gas and car repair station.[26] Every month, delegates were to report on road conditions in their area and on new developments in hotel, restaurant, and highway construction. The AMA National Council, with Montes de Oca as president and Rivera as secretary general, soon learned from another member, José Queralt Mir, that many of the newly formed delegations were uncooperative, not to mention unenthusiastic. A principal problem, according to reports, was suspicion. The AMA suggested that each group establish an office, whether in a local gas station or hotel. In Zimápan, for example, the owner of the gas station, Estación Mission, was afraid that the AMA's plans to develop tourism conflicted with those of prominent oil companies like Huasteca and Pierce, both with their own tourist departments.[27] The owner requested proof from managers of both oil companies that they were in cooperation, not in conflict, with the AMA. Other delegates simply refused to invest their time and money. They wanted reassurance from an AMA national member that their efforts would prove valuable.[28] As a result, Luis Montes de Oca set out on a four-day tour of the highway to meet with group members and to discuss their concerns.[29]

In addition to forming clubs across the republic, the AMA worked to establish tourist services along the border and in Mexico City.

From Monterrey, Antonio L. Rodríguez, local AMA president, began negotiations with members of the Laredo Chamber of Commerce to establish a tourist bureau that would offer promotional literature, exchange currency, and sell temporary AMA memberships as well as Mexican automobile insurance. The Consolidated Tourist Bureau opened for business on October 12, 1936, in Hotel Hamilton in Laredo, Texas. According to the agreement, AMA representative, Belisario A. Quiros, gave lectures on Mexico to potential tourists and sold temporary AMA memberships. The Bureau, financed by AMA funds, would advise tourists on Customs and Immigrations formalities and exchange currency at a fixed rate. Quiros was to submit daily financial reports to the AMA-Mexico City Club, the AMA-Monterrey Club and the Laredo Chamber of Commerce. Unfortunately, over the next year, the Bureau mishandled funds and maintained a deficit. In addition, a longstanding fight between the Mexican and American contingency for control over this tourist office emerged almost as soon as the office opened. Apparently, Quiros reported to the AMA-Monterrey Club that members of the Laredo Chamber of Commerce, even the secretary, with whom he shared the office, had no respect for him. To make matters worse, Rodríguez reported to the National Council that members of the Laredo Chamber of Commerce simply had no desire to sell tourism in Mexico and sought personal enrichment at financial cost to the AMA. This battle continued through 1938 when the National Council finally closed the Laredo office and opened a new one in Nuevo Laredo, Tamaulipas. On the Laredo, Texas side, the American Automobile Association, the cause of another fight after oil nationalization,[30] disseminated promotional materials to American tourists. In less than seven months, the AMA's Laredo office provided assistance to well over 4,000 motor tourists entering Mexico. The federal government gave the office a concession, though only temporarily, to grant tourist cards and temporary car permits. Agents at the office exchanged currency and sold tourist guides, insurance, and temporary memberships.[31] Inspired by the success in Laredo, in May 1937, the AMA opened an Office of Tourist Information in Mexico City in cooperation with the government's Department of Tourism.

The AMA increasingly offered services to its temporary and permanent members that not only provided them with travel guides, travel literature, and road maps, but also with emergency road assistance. Members also received a complementary copy of the magazine *MAPA*. Founded by Luis Montes de Oca through Editorial Mercurio, a publishing house run by Francisco Borja Bolado, *MAPA* was first published in 1934 under the direction of hotel expert, Lucas de Palacio. Not designed to attract foreign tourism per se, *MAPA* was a Spanish-language magazine that updated Mexican readers on recent highway and hotel developments as well as provided news from AMA delegations across the republic. Its writers frequently criticized the slow advancement of tourism. One author wrote in late 1936 that neither the authorities nor private individuals worked to develop tourism in Acapulco. There, she argued, tourists found horrible food, high hotel prices, and overall discomfort. She feared that they would equate the filth and backwardness (there were few streetlights) in Acapulco with something "typically Mexican."[32]

For motor tourists entering Mexico in 1936, the AMA published information on accommodations and services along the Nuevo Laredo-Mexico City Highway and in Mexico City. Over time, the AMA gained a long list of "affiliated members" that included hotels and motels, restaurants, curiosity stores, medical care, garages, and service stations. By 1937, the club offered discounts to tourists who stayed the night at affiliated hotels, parked their cars at affiliated garages, and drank at affiliated nightclubs. AMA National Council members, as pointed out earlier, began to compile these lists in summer 1936 after they inaugurated the highway. In the fall of that same year their list remained quite small, a reflection of the lack of hotels throughout the republic rather than a reflection of the AMA's connections. It included fifteen affiliated hotels in Mexico City, four in Monterrey, five in Guadalajara, three in Puebla, and fewer in places like Cuernavaca and Taxco. By July 1937, on the first anniversary of the Pan-American Highway's (note the official name change) inauguration, the list had nearly doubled, especially in Mexico City. This time, the AMA published a list of affiliated hotels broken down by number of rooms and services offered. They even appended a list, though short, of affiliated nightclubs in Mexico City. In just 1 year, their list expanded to 32 affiliated hotels in Mexico City, and 3 and 4 in Acapulco and Puebla. This boom in hotel construction can be traced, in part, to AMA members. Since 1936, AMA members organized clubs along the highway in an effort to mobilize local, private interest. Over time, affiliated members of the AMA throughout the republic represented the nation's most luxurious hotels and resorts including the renovated Hotel Geneve, Hotel Reforma, Hotel Mirador, Hotel Majestic, and María Cristina.

The AMA also worked to inspire owners and managers of affiliated hotels. Luis Montes de Oca often wrote letters to hotel owners with titles like, "Service, not Servitude." In letters like this, Montes de Oca explained that a successful tourist industry could rely on well-organized, reliable, and courteous service.[33] Tourists came to Mexico to see archaeological, architectural, and folkloric treasures, but in order to enjoy them they needed good service. He reminded readers that this in no way implied servitude, or the sacrifice of Mexican customs and authenticity to cater to tourists. Rather, he encouraged hotel owners to serve tourists with dignity, professionalism, and fairness.[34]

Not surprising, the financing for many of these hotels came from the same institutions on whose boards of directors sat Luis Montes de Oca. As president of the Mexican Banker's Association and director general of the Bank of Mexico, he was a central force in creating the Asociación Hipótecaria Mexicana (Mexican Mortgage Association) and the Sociedad de Crédito Hotelero (Hotel Credit Society), which began lending on September 1, 1938 with a total of Mex$18 million in hand.[35] These institutions lent capital to former president Pascual Ortíz Rubio's motel construction company, for example, and to Carlos Barnard, owner of Hotel El Mirador in Acapulco.

Through these lending institutions, Montes de Oca and his associates helped define the standards for future hotel construction. That is, they established a criterion for luxurious hotels in the capital and other principal cities and a criterion for more modest hotels in smaller towns and villages. According to this criterion, hotels in cities were to conform to the overarching architectural style and to Mexican tradition and art. Where no dominant style existed, developers were encouraged to choose a modern but modest (not strident) construction. Those planning to build hotels in towns and villages were directed to first study both climate and location in order to construct a hotel in the most picturesque or convenient spot.[36] The Hotel Credit Society also established standards for luxury, first- and second-class hotels. Luxury hotels should be exquisitely decorated rooms with a full bathroom including toilet, bathtub, and bidet with running hot and cold water; first-class hotel rooms were to have a shower and toilet only; and second-class hotels only a common bathroom area shared by all the rooms.[37]

The changes underway in hotel construction by 1938 should not be underestimated. The AMA and these lending institutions, under the guidance of Montes de Oca, provoked a boom in hotel construction and hotel renovation that transformed Mexico City by 1946. They also created a demand for organizations such as the Mexican Hotel Association (AMH), created in 1938 under the direction of Lucas de Palacio and Luis Osio Torres y Rivas, both members of the AMA.[38] Hoteliers, many who did not belong to any hotel association, formed the AMH and worked directly with the AMA, the future Mexican Tourist Association, and government-run tourist organizations. They soon published their own magazine entitled, *Hoteles Mexicanos*, and founded Mexico City's first hotel-training school in 1947, La Escuela Técnica Hotelera (known today as the Mexican Tourism School or EMT), that still exists today.[39] This school was founded through the cooperation of the Minister of National Economy Antonio Ruiz Galindo, and members of the AMH, especially Lucas de Palacio and Luis Osio y Torres Rivas. Minister Ruiz Galindo owned the fabulous Hotel Ruiz Galindo, known for its blooming gardenias located in Fortín de las Flores, Veracruz.

Efforts to develop Mexico's tourist industry played a central role in the proliferation of hotel construction. More than that, it reflected broader efforts by Mexico City planners during the Cárdenas era to construct what they believed to be the "real" Mexico. Patrice Olsen argues that the capital city embodied the contradictions of this period, contradictions inherent in an administration whose policies epitomized the revolution but whose architects destroyed evidence of that revolution by constructing buildings emblazoned with its colonial past or with modern styles.[40] As a result, city planners defined the "true Mexico" by what they thought tourists wanted to see, and, ultimately, excluded the revolutionary period. But was there a style of revolutionary Mexico? Perhaps these contradictions were the real expression of the "Mexico of the revolution". Throughout the 1930s, tourist promoters and developers, especially urban planners and hoteliers, debated the notion of an authentic Mexico. The government encouraged this debate found especially among members of the government-run National Tourism Committee (CTNT). Members' efforts to create new tourist attractions and to beautify Mexico point to the ways they defined *lo mexicano* (Mexican national identity). In the end, they and other groups agreed on the contradiction described earlier, and they sold Mexico as the embodiment of both modernity and antiquity.

DEFINING NATIONAL IDENTITY: THE CTNT

When José Quevedo, head of the government's Department of Tourism from 1936 to 1937 invited representatives from the private sector to join what became the National Tourism Committee (CTNT),[41] he included many members of the AMA. Under the state's wing, he expanded the network of tourist developers and promoters who would make the industry a success by the mid-1940s. Whereas the

AMA focused its efforts on providing services and accommodations, the CTNT turned its focus toward promotion. Quevedo gathered an impressive array of transportation, hotel, and oil interests as well as journalists and bankers for the first meeting held on September 17, 1936 in the offices of the Department of Tourism. Among those representing oil interests were AMA members Coleman and Flower, and E.V. Everson from Petróleo "El Aguila." Representatives from transportation included Rafael Mondrágon from Mexican Railways (Ferrocarril Mexicano), J.F. Orozco Escobosa from National Railways of Mexico (FFCCN), Hugo Cervantes from Missouri Pacific, Ricardo Noriega from M.K.T. Railways, J. Silva from Ward Line (Mexican subsidiary of New York & Cuba Mail Steamship Co.), Francisco Santacruz from Grace Line (steamship company), A. Penedo from Standard Fruit and Steamship Co., and Colonel Pedro A. Chapa from the Mexican Aviation Co. (owned by Aarón Sáenz Garza but a subsidiary of Pan American Airways). Invited banking and industrial interests included Luis Montes de Oca from his position as president of the Banker's Association, Firmin Fulda from the American Chamber of Commerce, and J. Rochin from the Confederation of Chambers of Commerce. Others present included Lucas de Palacio from the AMH, José Rivera R. from the AMA, Enrique Aguirre from Aguirre's Guest Tours, F. Libau from Wells Fargo's Travel Department, Humberto Valencia Solis from the newspaper *Excélsior*, and five officials from the government's Department of Tourism.[42] Over the next few years, membership in the CTNT expanded to include prominent figures like former president Pascual Ortíz Rubio, Aarón Sáenz Garza, radio and television mogul Emilio Azcárraga, and Frank Sanborn of Sanborn's Restaurant.

CTNT members spent much of their time at meetings discussing the direction for their projects. Like its predecessors, the government's motivation for bringing together prominent representatives from the private sector was to mobilize energies toward the development and promotion of tourism. Despite the fact that the federal government had done little to this point to develop tourism, apart from border policies and conservation laws, the CTNT served as an important forum in which the government could direct the industry's development. At their first meeting, Committee President José Quevedo, using nationalistic rhetoric, gave a speech that outlined three focus areas: tourist promotion, services, and attractions. From the time when the government made this industry official in 1929, developers consistently discussed the first two, but Quevedo broached a new topic with the issue of tourist attractions. This part of his speech raised a series of topics related to, among other things, national identity. In so doing, Quevedo set the tone for future CTNT projects that focused on defining Mexican-ness. According to Quevedo, tourism placed Mexico in a cruel paradox, a paradox that historically corrupted things typically Mexican.[43] He argued that as towns and cities introduced new diversions and foods modeled on the foreign in an effort to appeal to tourists, Mexican customs and traditions slowly degenerated. If tourist developers followed this trajectory, he feared, the nation's soul would die. As a solution, he proposed that the CTNT develop tourist attractions such as regional fairs, popular festivals, and typical music and dance that vigorously defended what he believed to be the essence of Mexico. While he did not completely dismiss foreign spectacles that had some educative element like opera, theatre, ballet, and the symphony, he impressed upon committee members the idea of developing "moral" tourist attractions that did not corrupt national identity and, instead, fomented native arts.[44]

Quevedo echoed concerns that government officials had expressed only years before especially when they studied Cuba's tourist industry in the late 1920s and found that foreigners largely developed and owned it. The question surrounding how Mexican leaders could reconcile the promotion of their nation to American tourists without losing what they believed the revolution had accomplished remained central to their debates about the industry's development. The moral character of Quevedo's speech about upholding and selling national identity was shaped in large part by the revolutionary creed rooted not only in economic and cultural nationalism, but also in the desire for internationalism—international recognition and a role in global affairs.[45] Unlike the Porfirian era (1876–1910), members of the revolutionary elite who represented official and private sectors sought to gain international recognition by controlling the means of production, by directing the development of industry, and by retaining profits in Mexico and in Mexican hands. With his speech, Quevedo struck a patriotic chord with committee members and ultimately encouraged them to debate definitions of Mexican national identity.

Through their proposed and completed projects over the next few years, CTNT members began to define national culture as the convergence of modernity and antiquity. Rather than a paradox, these dichotomies suited overarching revolutionary goals. At the first meeting, Orozco Escobosa told the committee that while living in the United States he learned that Americans equated Mexicans with savages.[46] The kinds of suggestions members made to reverse this impression points to the ways in which these tourist pioneers came to define modernity and modern Mexico. For Colonel Chapa of Mexicana Airlines, modernity meant sanitation and hygiene. He argued that the government should "clean house" to ensure the health of tourists. To do this, government officials should provide potable water to towns throughout the republic as well as inspect restaurants, motels, and hotels.[47] Other members seconded this proposal but added that the government should ensure that tourists not see vagrants and beggars on streets and along the railroads. This, they argued, gave tourists the worst impression of Mexico.[48]

CTNT members equated modernity with leisure and diversion, especially the potential for an active nightlife in Mexico City. One member submitted a study based on what tourists did in Canada in 1936 to show that tourists spent their dollars on food, accommodation, and fun. He argued that Mexico City had no nightlife but if developed tourists would spend an estimated US$10 per night at cabarets and bars.[49] By October 1937, a representative of Mexico City's nightclubs, Manuel del Valle, was invited to join the "Organized Commission of Pro-Tourism Popular Festivals," a section of the Committee that sought to develop attractions by organizing seasonal and permanent "typical festivals."[50] Members recognized the role nightlife played not only in attracting tourists, but also in constructing an image of a cosmopolitan capital city. They argued against Quevedo and his morality, and opted for the best of both worlds. One member wrote that the tourist needed ambience: to listen to folkloric music at a nightclub.[51]

Members defined one aspect of modernity as the conservation of the past coupled with programs of urban renewal. The CTNT's projected program for 1937 sought to pass a series of laws including the "Conservation Law of Monuments and Natural Beauty," the "Planning and Conservation Law of Cities and Towns," the "Planning Law of the Countryside," the "Forestry Law," the "Law of National Parks," as well as laws that regulated space, hotel construction, and architectural style.[52] The government made great strides in protecting Mexico's national monuments, buildings, and historical objects. Ratified into law in January 1937, this "Law to Protect Artistic and Historic Treasures of Mexico," sought to preserve all archaeological ruins and objects dated before 1521 as well as all buildings, art, and material objects dated from 1521 to 1821. The law created a panel of university professors, government officials, local art historians, and representatives of historical societies who determined the objects of historical or artistic interest worthy of protection under this law. The federal government, according to this law, could reclaim those "national treasures" for which individuals did not properly care.[53] CTNT members as well as other groups argued that efforts to protect Mexico's past could only succeed when coupled with efforts to improve the present.

The CTNT was not alone in debating definitions of national culture through urban renewal and beautification projects. In fact, years earlier, in 1930, architects and engineers who attended a Planning Congress defended the "typical character" of towns and villages as something Mexican nationals and foreign tourists alike found especially attractive.[54] One participant argued that tourists wanted to see authentic Mexico in comfort and with amenities. For example, he asserted that tourists wanted to see Mexico's tropical forests without mosquitoes biting them, that they wanted to drive on picturesque roads with gasoline stations, and that they wanted to enjoy Mexico's beaches of fine sand at accommodations of luxurious hotels "with casinos, with racetracks and with all the comforts of modern life."[55] Participants presented beautification projects, especially for Mexico City. Forestry experts Ángel Roldan and Miguel Ángel de Quevedo suggested that gardens and parks be built around the city as well as trees planted along city streets to combat the grave consequences of urbanization. Trees such as eucalyptus and jacaranda could be used to beautify neighborhoods and streets as well as provide a source of oxygen in an increasingly congested capital.[56] These experts were certainly correct in their suggestions. Their plans were carried out especially in neighborhoods like Colonia Roma and Colonia Hipódromo.[57] Finally, one engineer suggested that the only way to beautify the capital was to regulate street vending by licensing newspaper and lottery ticket vendors, by ridding (from plain sight) beggars and vagrants, and by closing *pulquerias*. This, he argued, would create a moral capital city where agreeable, civilized people could live.[58]

In addition to members of the Planning Congress, the Mexico City government (Departamento del Distrito Federal, or DDF) was also active in urban planning when in spring 1932 it hired French Urbanist and Technical Consultant Jacques H. Lambert to conduct a series of studies to beautify the capital. From April to June, Lambert studied the Plaza de Constitución, and the city's main thoroughfares like Avenida "20 de Noviembre," to, among other reasons, determine ways to improve the flow of traffic through the historic center in and around the *Zócalo* (central plaza). Officials asked him to study the question of skyscrapers that would guide future regulatory construction policies. His avid supporter Luis Montes de Oca reviewed his reports submitted in French.[59] By the summer, Lambert filed his reports and left amid negative reactions to his studies. According to Montes de Oca, the attacks on Lambert were rooted in rampant nativism rather than his abilities as an urban planer.[60] Ironically, when Mexico City planners began again to study beautification and renewal projects in 1936, they reviewed Lambert's reports. While they described his suggestions as magnificent, they argued that they were architecturally too European and not within the Mexican tradition.[61]

What exactly defined a Mexican traditional style was once again discussed by planners in 1936 as it related to the influx of American tourists in Mexico, especially motorists who passed through Nuevo Laredo. The government's Department of Tourism even circulated a letter to all local officials encouraging them to make necessary improvements so that tourists felt comfortable while visiting Mexico. Written by José Quevedo, who advocated a "healthy and intelligently organized" tourist industry, local officials were encouraged to conserve paved roads and construct new ones, build gardens, construct hotels and buildings that were not discordant with local architectural style, and to organize events that preserved *lo típico* (the typical).[62] As the point of entry for motorists traveling on the new Nuevo Laredo–Mexico City Highway, the city of Nuevo Laredo received planners' attention. While they carried out few projects, what emerged out of these plans points to the ways architects and engineers in the 1930s defined Mexican national identity.

The government, AMA, banking institutions, architects, and engineers discussed the organization of a Planning Commission in Nuevo Laredo. Formed at the close of 1936 on the initiative of Luis Montes de Oca and President Cárdenas, its supporters argued that problems found at the border were urgent. Unlike concerns of the late 1920s and early 1930s that focused on border entry policies, these were matters of aesthetics. The fact remained that motor tourists had to be lured to the heart of Mexico—its capital city. This, according to many, was difficult when motorists crossed the International Bridge to Nuevo Laredo to find a town broken down, a river contaminated, and streets congested. Architect Vicente Mendiola Q. described the city as "heterogeneous" and "smelly" with "nothing architecturally beautiful."[63] If that were not enough, he described buildings in Nuevo Laredo as "a hybrid of forms and of American style." More than the pungent smell found in Nuevo Laredo, this was an insult to all border cities that had fallen victim to "gringoization" or what some at the time referred to as *tijuanización* (or the Tijuana effect).[64] To suffer from this meant that Nuevo Laredo lacked Mexican character. He argued that little evidence of an authentic Mexican culture, tradition, or style could be found in Nuevo Laredo's architecture and in its attractions that featured gambling, prostitution, and liquor. Once corrected, Mendiola argued, tourists could exit the bridge at Nuevo Laredo and immediately feel and understand Mexico. According to this city planner, "authentic" Mexico was rooted in its recent, revolutionary progress (Mexican-made modernity) and in its past (colonial and indigenous antiquity).

For six months, architects and engineers of the Nuevo Laredo Planning Commission studied the layout of this border city and in July 1937 proposed a Mex$5.7 million improvement project. They planned to construct or at least renovate the international point (the point at which one arrived on Mexican soil and was met by customs agents). At the international point, they hoped to construct a new building for tourist services, including toilets and travel information, and to offer new customs facilities. In the city of Nuevo Laredo, they planned to expand potable water lines and planned an ambitious construction project that would include new federal and municipal buildings, a secondary school, four primary schools, a hospital, a market and flea market, and a park with lighted fountain. Finally, they planned to pave, illuminate, and beautify the Avenida Lerdo, the avenue that led to the Pan-American Highway, and to pave the "old city."[65] Planners set aside a total of Mex$875,000 to renovate the "old city," Mex$600,000 to construct a new international point, Mex$480,000 to build new government buildings, and Mex$410,000 to beautify Lerdo Avenue.

Based on this proposal and its budget, planners had a clear vision for the kind of image they wanted to present to potential tourists. First, they wanted to lure motorists to Nuevo Laredo's historical center, perhaps the city's only remnant of history that reflected a typical Mexican style. Furthermore, they hoped to renovate the International Bridge first constructed in 1887 and later rebuilt after a devastating fire in the 1920s. In both cases, American businesses provided most of the capital to construct the bridge. As a result, planners argued, its builders took little care to beautify the bridge once it touched Mexican soil.[66] Planners hoped to construct new, hygienic government buildings in an effort to place strong and healthy symbols of Mexico in motorists' plain view. Finally, by beautifying the route that led motorists to the Pan-American Highway they hoped to attract the kind of tourist with only the best intentions, namely those who did not patronize Nuevo Laredo's cabarets, cantinas, and centers of vice. Taken together, efforts to tempt tourists to see authentic Mexico lay not only in the border city's historic center, but also in Mexico

City. Urban planners and tourist developers invested their hopes and capital for a successful tourist industry in the "City of Palaces." In so doing, it came to embody the essence of Mexican identity.

COMBATING DISASTER: HURRICANES, OIL, AND BAD PRESS

While AMA members were busy organizing delegations across the republic, and while CTNT members and planning commissions debated the essence of an authentic Mexico, friends of Mexico in the United States worked to promote that nation as an ideal tourist destination. This task would repeatedly prove to be Mexico's greatest challenge in building this national industry. As chapters 1 and 2 point out, prevailing impressions about Mexico held by potential American tourists were hardly flattering. With the exception of the AMA, tourist pioneers spent little money and even less time promoting Mexico in the United States. Once the war in Europe broke out in 1939, promotion became central to tourist development. As before, Mexican tourist boosters from 1936 to 1938 relied on their contacts in the United States to change impressions about "barbaric" Mexico. Unfortunately, it seemed that with every step forward, something happened in Mexico to set back promotional campaigns. These disasters, one natural and one intentional, coincided with one another to produce a wave of negative press about Mexico throughout the United States. Thanks to William H. Furlong, longtime advocate of Mexico who also happened to be on the AMA's payroll, tourist rates to Mexico only temporarily dropped. More importantly, tourist pioneers learned that advertising through the mass media was the best way to gain the attention of Americans. Bad press about Mexico did not necessarily hinge upon natural disasters or attacks on American-owned oil companies. On the eve of the Pan-American Highway's one-year anniversary, the *New York Times* published an article entitled, "To Mexico by Motor," written by Thelma and Blinn Yates. Far from laudatory, this article warned motorists about potential problems they faced when traveling to Mexico City along this international highway. According to the authors, they found no potable water anywhere. The "road" was unfinished, and the result was high traffic due to construction work by steamrollers and trucks. They warned motorists about highway dangers because it lacked guardrails. Sections went unpaved so that drivers "tempted fate" when traveling over 25 miles per hour. And, finally, grazing cattle, sheep, pigs, goats, chickens, and sleeping dogs impeded a smooth ride.[67]

One man, Texan William H. Furlong, almost immediately came to the defense of Mexico's newest modern highway. In a letter to the travel editor, George Copeland, Furlong wrote that the authors' depiction of Mexico was entirely inaccurate and outdated. He admitted that some years earlier, motorists made an unwise decision when they drank Mexican water and ate food along the highway. He agreed that only a year earlier it would have been impossible to find a hotel where one could enjoy a good night's sleep. According to Furlong, times had changed. Vast improvements had been made in tourist accommodations and services, especially comfortable lodging, potable water, tasty food, and clean surroundings. His letter went to such lengths as to describe the food motorists would find at the Hotel Casa Grande in Valles, where, for example, the restaurant served a typical American meal of broiled chicken, soup, salad, potatoes, and dessert. Furlong continued to write that motorists could expect to find a breakfast of ham and eggs, hotcakes and coffee in Huichihuan as well as Del Monte tinned products and Libby's tinned tongue and corned beef at the Hotel Mante in Villa Juárez.[68] Finally, to prove to the editor that the Yates's article was inaccurate, he invited Copeland to view a film, see photographs, and hear a lecture about the Pan-American Highway at Furlong's hotel in New York City the week of May 17. Auspiciously, Furlong had been invited to New York to give a presentation on Mexico's highways at the Automobile Manufacturers Association's "Foreign Trade Week."[69]

As his letter demonstrates, Furlong provided an invaluable service to the AMA and to the overall growth of Mexico's tourist industry. He not only defended the safety and comfort of motor travel to Mexico, but he also promoted Mexico throughout the United States by giving presentations and by publishing "The Furlong Service," an English-language newsletter that provided information about Mexico's highway conditions and highway projects.[70] More than just a report on the state of that nation's roads, "The Furlong Service" provided U.S. motorists with a guide to specific hotel, motels, restaurants, and gas and repair stations, each AMA affiliated. This newsletter also provided a reassuring voice to apprehensive motor tourists who entered Mexico for the first time. Active in road building since the 1920s, Furlong worked from the St. Anthony Hotel in San Antonio, Texas where delegates from the Road Commission founded the AMA in 1929. He served as U.S. representative to Mexico's National Road Commission, secretary of the Inter-American Highway Association (devoted to building the Inter-American Highway, a.k.a. Pan-American

Highway), founding associate member and employee of the AMA, and for a time, employee of Mexico's official Department of Tourism and the privately funded Mexican Tourist Association.

Whereas the costs to publish "The Furlong Service" were fairly minimal—it was printed on typed sheets of paper—the costs to fund Furlong's inspections along Mexico's highways were expensive but well worth it. Every few months Furlong took a trip along the Nuevo Laredo-Mexico City Highway to update his readers on the latest conditions and accommodations. Following the highway's opening, he began to include in the "Furlong Service" a list of hotels and motels motorists would find on their way to Monterrey as well as desirable rest stops further south. He urged tourists to carry along folding cots with mosquito nets, canned foods, and bottled water because accommodations and services along the highway were still "under construction."[71] Furlong frequently invited journalists and motor club presidents to see Mexico's progress firsthand. Increasingly after 1936, often in cooperation with the AMA and Mexico's National Road Commission, he took U.S. journalists and executive members of motor clubs on personal highway tours. These tours served as promotional tools; the investments paid off with agreements to publish positive press about Mexico. In early 1937, Furlong allowed Russell Gordon, Sunday editor of the *Boston Herald*, and Frank L. Perrin, writer from *Christian Science Monitor* to accompany him on a tour of Mexico's highways. By early summer, both journalists wrote praiseworthy articles on motor tourism in Mexico.[72] In the summer of 1937, Furlong accompanied a group of women journalists, including the fashion editor from the *Detroit Times*, on a tour of Mexico's highways. In letters of thanks to him, one journalist noted how courteous José Rivera R. was in sending her a basket of violets and honoring her with an AMA membership.[73] In another letter, journalist Dorothy Smith expressed her hope that the *Detroit Times* "can help give the proper sort of publicity to your adopted country in the weeks and months to come [that] will induce many, many more Americans to go to Mexico."[74]

Furlong toured the United States giving a series of presentations using film and photographs to promote motor tourism in Mexico as another way to combat bad press and forge alliances with journalists and automobile club presidents. In Detroit, he attended an American Automobile Association (AAA) meeting and met with its executive committee members as well as with journalists and publicists from the *Detroit Times*, *Detroit News*, *Automobile News*,

Automobile Club of Michigan, and the marketing agency Campbell, Ewald & Co. In Dearborn, Michigan, he met with the director of Ford Exhibits and the secretary to Henry Ford, and presented his lecture to executives, employees, and schoolchildren of the Ford Motor Company in the Ford Theatre; while there, he even met Henry Ford. Moreover, in St. Louis, he met with travel writers from the *St. Louis Globe-Democrat, St. Louis Star Times*, and other newspapers.[75] These tours, which Furlong continued to make well into the 1940s, proved beneficial to the AMA and Mexico's tourist industry in general. He informed the Automobile Association of the good press that usually followed his meetings by reprinting news stories in "The Furlong Service." At times, he also published a list of recommended readings like Anita Brenner's *Your Mexican Holiday* or Phillip Terry's *Guide to Mexico*.[76] By 1937, Furlong's efforts won publicity (text and photographs) for Mexico in prominent American newspapers and magazines, a few of which included the following: *New York Times, New Orleans Times-Picayune, Boston Herald, Chicago Tribune, Denver Post, The Enquirer, Collier's, Newsweek*, and *Pan American Bulletin*.[77]

Lucky for the AMA and other tourist developers in Mexico, when disaster struck in late 1937 and again in 1938, Furlong's labors toward tourist promotion were well on their way to being successful. In early November 1937, President Cárdenas expropriated 350,000 acres of Standard Oil land, the first in subsequent moves to nationalize oil in Mexico. In an announcement over the radio, Cárdenas told the nation on March 18, 1938 that the federal government had expropriated all U.S.- and British-owned oil companies.[78] While ordinary Mexicans expressed their overwhelming support for nationalization by donating whatever money and jewelry they had for reparations, the American press corps, and of course oil companies, were outraged.

Oil nationalization certainly damaged, at least temporarily, Mexico's tourist industry. Almost immediately, tourist entries through Nuevo Laredo fell to half of what they had been the year before.[79] A deluge of condemnations circulated throughout the United States. To make matters worse, Standard Oil affiliates like Continental Oil (Conoco) and Texas Oil (Texaco) began to publish warnings about motor travel to Mexico as part of a broader anti-Mexico campaign choreographed by publicist Steve Hanagan.[80] Whereas both companies had produced promotional literature and maps about motoring to Mexico only months earlier, they spread rumors after oil nationalization that there were gasoline shortages and anti-American sentiment south of the border. One witness found an announcement posted in Houston,

Texas gas stations that stated the following:

> Special Bulletin:
>
> We are enclosing our new 1938 map of Mexico purely as a matter of interest. The trip is definitely not recommended since all tourist traffic to that country has practically ceased. As you will doubtless wish to change your vacation plans, we are enclosing a routing request card for your use.[81]

Additional reports poured into AMA and AMH offices expressing concern about the negative press. High school teacher Mary B. Bookmeyer from Omaha, Nebraska wrote directly to William Furlong to ask for reassurance about a motor trip she and four other teachers had planned to Mexico along the Pan-American Highway. She requested his reassurance that travel was safe, despite the oil companies' warnings not to go.[82]

Furlong and others acted quickly to tell the real story about the state of Mexico's highways following oil nationalization. In late April, he broadcasted a radio show that was played on stations from Memphis to St. Louis. Its goal was to combat rumors about the dangers of travel to Mexico by addressing misnomers about oil and gasoline shortages, lack of modern tourist accommodations, dangerous road conditions, and Mexican hostility toward Americans. Listeners learned that at no time since expropriation was there ever a danger or problem facing tourists who traveled by air, road, sea, or railway. Moreover, he reassured them that there was ample gasoline, adequate accommodations, and a highway entirely paved from Texas to Mexico City. Finally, from his profound experience of travel throughout Mexico, he assured listeners that in Mexico people had only treated him with heartfelt friendliness and goodwill. U.S. tourists, he concluded, could anticipate an enjoyable vacation and a genuine welcome.[83] In addition, the new director of the Department of Tourism, Abraham Mejía, did his part when he drove from Mexico City to Texas to assure the public that motor travel was both safe and gas-plenty. He even asked President Cárdenas if he could continue his tour all the way to California.[84] Fortunately, much of the damage to Mexico's reputation after expropriation was reversible. By August, Furlong sent word to officials that Conoco and Texaco had withdrawn their warnings about travel to Mexico.[85] Even though Ambassador Josephus Daniels refused the Mexican Minister of Foreign Affairs Eduardo Hay's request to take action against the rumors spread by American oil companies, tourist rates began to improve by late summer 1938 only to slow again after rumors about a hurricane and flood that stranded 1,000 U.S. tourists in San Luis Potosí.[86]

Conflicting stories surrounded this natural disaster. According to AMA reports, Mexican organizations had taken every measure to ensure the safety of American tourists. When José Rivera R. received news about a hurricane making its way to Mexico on August 29, the AMA sent warnings about potentially hazardous driving conditions to all hotels and tourist centers throughout the republic. In Mexico City, AMH-affiliated hotels including the Hotel Imperial, Guardiola, Ontario, Ritz, Reforma, Regis, L'Escargot, Majestic, and Carlton offered 20 percent discounts on hotel rates to tourists unable to travel home. Moreover, the FFCCN (National Railways of Mexico) offered 50 percent discounted railway fares to tourists and their cars in an effort to return them safely to the United States.[87] The Mexican Red Cross provided assistance for an estimated 500 tourists stranded in San Luis Potosí. Reports showed that the CTNT, FFCCN, National Road Commission, AMH, U.S. Embassy and Consulate, and the Red Cross cooperated to improve the situation.[88] Nevertheless, rumors spread throughout the American press about tourists stranded with diminishing food and water supplies.[89]

Reactions to the hurricane by tourists supposedly stranded in Mexico and those by the U.S. press varied. On the one hand, a group of 30 tourists wrote a letter of appreciation to the AMA and FFCCN for the courtesy they were shown during this disaster. The American Automobile Association even sent the AMA a telegram congratulating them on the swift and safe return of U.S. tourists.[90] On the other hand, one stranded tourist, Hal Worth of Dallas, told the San Antonio press that as many as 1,500 tourists were stranded, many of them ill from drinking contaminated water and many of them starving from dwindling food supplies. He also informed the press of the incompetence of Mexican officials who, when they did not make the repairs as promised, he accused of as misleading him to believe that the bridge near Valles "would be repaired *mañana.*"[91]

As rumors spread about the one thousand or more starving and ill tourists, William Furlong's earlier efforts to combat bad press and to spread good news about tourism in Mexico appeared to pay off. On September 3, radio broadcaster Miss Gay from KMOX, "The Voice of St. Louis," interviewed the station's program director C.G. Renier about road conditions in Mexico. She described to listeners the recent weather conditions that damaged bridges along the Pan-American Highway and stranded tourists. She introduced Renier as a reliable source because he had recently returned from a tour along the highway with William Furlong, the station's guest in the spring. During his visit, Furlong had invited Renier to join him for a personal motor tour along Mexico's most modern highway. In light of Furlong's recent appearance on KMOX and Renier's recent tour in Mexico, it should come as no surprise that his answers tried to reverse prevailing impressions about the dangers of tourist travel to Mexico. Miss Gay's line of questioning begged for such praiseworthy answers. Renier emphasized that he found it hard to believe that tourists were suffering, especially considering the modern hotels in Ciudad Valles. When asked if there was anything serious about being stranded there, he remarked: "Oh yes, quite serious, it might mean a few of them will get a few extra days vacation."[92] Renier used the interview to make light of the situation, to reassure listeners that reports about stranded tourists were exaggerated, and to tout travel to Mexico in general. In the course of his interview, he mentioned that the Pan-American Highway was the pride of Mexico and, thus, well maintained and fully paved with modern amenities and great restaurants. Indeed, Renier's answers resonated with William H. Furlong's own presentations on motoring to Mexico.

* * *

When disaster struck in late 1937, William H. Furlong, the AMA's advocate, proved invaluable. Since 1936, Furlong had reported on road conditions in Mexico to American motor tourists through the "Furlong Service." He had also begun to tour the United States with films and photographs in tow to educate the public about Mexico's new international highway. While tourist developers and urban planners began to build the infrastructure of a national industry that presented an image of Mexican national identity, the promotion of tourism to Mexico through advertisement in the mass media emerged as another main ingredient in the overarching recipe for success. With Europe on the brink of war in 1939, Mexico's tourist pioneers banded together and seized the opportunity to sell their brand of authentic Mexico to U.S. tourists. As tourist markets in Europe vanished, the race for the tourist dollar moved closer to home. Tourist developers soon learned that they had to wait for the real profits from tourism because their target market weakened when the United States declared war on Axis powers in late 1941. Nevertheless, the strong push from 1939 to 1942 to promote tourism to Mexico through the mass media reflected more than Mexican society in transition. It reflected a growing friendship between two previously contentious neighbors. On this, Mexico's tourist promoters capitalized.

CHAPTER 4

"VACATIONING WITH A PURPOSE": TOURISM PROMOTION ON THE EVE OF WORLD WAR II

On the eve of World War II, Mexico's reputation in the United States dramatically shifted from an unruly to a good neighbor. Although tourist promoters had tried for years, with some success, to counteract negative press about Mexico, they had difficulty winning the trust of many. However, by late 1940 Americans seemed to replace their distrust with goodwill toward Mexico. They dismissed earlier rumors about growing anti-Americanism south of the border following President Lázaro Cárdenas's decision to nationalize foreign-owned oil companies, and overlooked unfounded reports about a brewing revolution in light of upcoming elections. Ordinary Americans began to embrace Mexico as "The Faraway Land Nearby"[1] and to identify a vacation there with the larger, almost spiritual purpose, namely to foster good relations. In unprecedented numbers, U.S. tourists like Dorothy Reinke traveled south following President Franklin D. Roosevelt's advice to take part in the new Inter-American travel movement. Dorothy, a 28-year-old nurse from Oklahoma City, drove coast-to-coast through Mexico with her girlfriend. In 1941, Dorothy wrote to President Manuel Ávila Camacho and described her experience in Mexico as transforming for her, "a sister from the north." She not only found Mexicans kind and friendly, and the climate and food far superior to anything in Canada, but she also met Roberto who showed her that romance transcended language and cultural differences. Much to her surprise, she found love and goodwill inside a package labeled "Mexican Vacation."[2]

While not everyone who traveled to Mexico would find romance as did Dorothy, many of the 166,000 persons who traveled by car and train in 1941 did arrive as emissaries of goodwill with the express intention to somehow play a role in creating hemispheric solidarity and understanding between two previously fractured nations. Tourism, many argued from both sides of the border, emerged as the ideal medium for this kind of cultural and economic exchange. In contrast to other Latin American nations, nearby Mexico was easy to reach by car or by train. Further, Mexico produced oil and other wartime goods (cottonseed oil and cheap labor) that the United States needed. Without access to European and Asian markets, U.S. officials looked to its Latin American neighbors, especially Mexico, to satisfy demands for raw materials. In so doing, the U.S. government, and other institutions that dealt with Latin America such as the Pan-American Union and the Office of Inter-American Affairs (OIAA), played their part in reshaping American attitudes toward Mexico.[3] Hollywood did too. By 1944, film companies distributed newsreels to American picture houses that showed footage of Mexico's political and economic progress. By 1946, MGM produced the musical, *Holiday in Mexico*, starring Jane Powell, Walter Pigeon, and Xavier Cugat and his orchestra. Mexico was not just in vogue by 1946 but it became such a household name that postwar tourist rates increased 100 percent over its best year in 1941.[4] Finally, as historians such as John Hart, Stephen Niblo, and Julio Moreno have shown, the U.S. government and corporate interests learned a great lesson from Cárdenas's efforts to nationalize industries in the late 1930s, namely that Mexicans wanted to control their own economic development and national industries; as a result, American interests towed a new line of collaboration with Mexico rather than conflict.[5]

How Mexico's reputation dramatically shifted from the barbaric to the good neighbor proves to be much more complex because neither Hollywood nor Nelson Rockefeller's Office of Inter-American Affairs (OIAA) nor Roosevelt's presidential decree were solely responsible for the change in reputation and the incredible influx of tourists to Mexico by 1946. Instead, Mexico's revolutionary elite as tourist promoters used the increasing importance of goodwill to further their own goals. These promoters, many of whom had been involved in developing this industry since the late 1920s, formed part of the newly established Mexican Tourist Association (AMT). More than any Mexican organization, the AMT remade Mexico's image. With financial support from Mexico's government ministries and almost all private businesses that benefited from tourism, the AMT flooded the

United States with publicity beginning in 1939, and continued to do so, even after Pearl Harbor and after oil and rubber rations made motoring to Mexico difficult during World War II. Through skillful campaigns in the U.S. press, radio, and film, Mexico's tourist promoters used to their advantage the increasing importance of goodwill. Members of the AMT not only produced tourist brochures, music programs, and press releases meant to promote a holiday in Mexico as a "vacation with a purpose,"[6] but they also organized meetings and excursions such as the 1941 "Presidential Tour" that brought American journalists and automobile club presidents to Mexico for a two-week, all-expense-paid trip. The benefits from these campaigns were priceless. One Ohio journalist and "Presidential Tour" participant, speaking on behalf of his fellow participants, told Mexico City's governor: "We will not only tell the folks back home that Mexico is the ideal vacation land . . . we will tell them that here one breathes the same invigorating air which makes mankind instinctively understand the value of friendship and true democracy."[7]

Indeed World War II put a damper on the sustained growth that Mexico's tourist industry had begun to enjoy. Although U.S. tourists found ways to fulfill Roosevelt's wish that ordinary Americans vacation to relieve wartime stress,[8] the hopes of many tourism promoters were dashed when the momentum with which tourism increased by 1941 fell substantially after the Japanese attack on Pearl Harbor. Nevertheless, Mexico took the lead over its greatest rivals, Canada and Cuba, in the competition for tourists that was in full swing by 1939. With help from American government and corporate interests as well as friends of Mexico, tourist promoters successfully transformed their nation's image. Timing was crucial in this story about the making of Mexico's tourist industry. Just as the United States began to rely on Mexico for wartime goods and for the defense of the new and common democratic front, tourist promoters inundated Americans with expressions of good neighborliness. Even before President Ávila Camacho openly declared Mexico's alliance with allied powers in 1942 by declaring war and by sending Squadron 201 to fight in the Philippines in 1944, Mexico's tourist promoters galvanized their efforts to ride the wave of goodwill.

WAR AND PEACE: PUBLICITY AND THE AMT

Mexico's tourist advocates from both official and private sectors understood that the promotion of travel to Mexico in the United States was central to the industry's success. Since the late 1920s, tourist organizations had been unable to fund the kind of advertising campaign needed to reverse long-standing negative press and deeply held negative impressions by many Americans about Mexico. By 1937, however, the government began to take a financial interest in the importance of advertising in the mass media when Cárdenas created the Department of Press and Publicity (DAPP). While little is known about the personnel and budget supporting DAPP, incorporated in 1940 into the Ministry of Interior's *Dirección General de Información* (Office of Intformation), it was the first official department responsible for producing and distributing propaganda in favor of Mexico and its government.[9] Among its many projects, DAPP produced and distributed an English-language, tourist guidebook and magazine on Mexico. In its first year, employees wrote and published a brochure entitled "The Valley of Mexico" with a colorful front cover of an Indian next to a snow-peaked volcano and a cactus.[10] Meant to illustrate to American readers symbols of Mexico's social and environmental composition that, the author contended, had been incorporated into the valley's modern life, these images were juxtaposed with a foldout map of the Valley of Mexico with Mexico City as the center of all outlying routes to Puebla, Cuernavaca, Acapulco, Querétaro, and elsewhere.[11] The next year, DAPP published the English-language tourist magazine, *Mexican Art & Life*. This quarterly magazine with beautifully designed, full-color covers executed by prominent artists ran for seven issues from 1937 to 1938. Finally, in 1939, the secretary general of DAPP, José Rivera, published a text entitled *Publicidad turística de México*, a tool geared toward tourist associations, as his department's contribution to the Rotary Club's Technical Congress on Tourism held in Mexico City from March 20 to March 25.[12]

Despite the publicity produced by DAPP and other organizations like the Mexican Automobile Association (AMA), it was simply not enough to combat disasters like those that took place in 1938, namely the hurricane that wiped out bridges along the Pan-American Highway and oil nationalization. After an unprecedented year in 1937 in which more than 130,000 Americans chose Mexico as their holiday destination, President Lázaro Cárdenas and U.S. Ambassador to Mexico Josephus Daniels celebrated the industry's success by appearing together in a full-page advertisement in *The Miami Herald* entitled, "The United States of the Republic of Mexico Wish you a Merry Christmas!" and what followed included signed 13 × 18 photographs of each, a series of articles on Christmas in Mexico, two published letters to journalist Arthur Perper written by Cárdenas and Daniels, images of Morelia, the Monument to Independence, and Uxmal ruins, and an advertisement by the National Railways of Mexico.[13] To Floridians, Cárdenas sent reassuring words. He explained that his administration and nation welcomed American tourists not only for its economic benefits to Mexico, but also because travel was the new vehicle for promoting mutual understanding between nations. Daniels reiterated this by adding that all U.S. tourists to Mexico "returned as Ambassadors of Good Will and friendship."[14] He concluded by encouraging readers to take part in what he expected to be a record-setting year of tourism in 1938.

Unfortunately, the ambassador's prediction proved wrong. Immediately following the news in March 1938 that President Cárdenas had expropriated all foreign-owned oil companies in Mexico, U.S. tourist entries dropped by half. Two oil companies, Texas Oil (Texaco) and Continental Oil (Conoco), spread rumors about the dangers of travel to Mexico. They warned motorists that Mexicans were increasingly anti-American, that they would experience gas shortages along the Pan-American Highway, and that the new government-run oil company, Petróleos Mexicanos (Pemex), produced low-grade gasoline and oil that was harmful to American automobiles. To make matters worse, just as the tourist traffic began to recover, a natural disaster blew into Mexico in late summer destroying bridges along the Pan-American Highway. The nation's tourist organizations quickly rallied to reverse the damage caused by these otherwise natural disasters. AMA's Texas representative, William H. Furlong, continued his active lecture tour across the United States to combat bad press through education about Mexico's highways and hotels. Since 1936, Furlong had been meeting with auto club presidents, journalists, travel agents, and ordinary Americans in an effort to sell the idea of motor travel on Mexico's highways. While on tour, he not only presented a lecture but also used forms of mass media to replace ignorance with knowledge. He presented color film footage of Mexico's roads and frequently gave radio interviews. At each stop, he made sure to invite journalists and auto club presidents to accompany him on a personal tour of Mexico's highways. Many accepted the invitation and, upon their return, published laudatory articles about tourism to Mexico. As the nation's liaison in the United States, Furlong indeed forged relationships that transformed ordinary men and women into "Ambassadors of Goodwill" toward Mexico.[15] In another effort, members of the Hotel Greeters of Mexico led by Antonio Pérez O. (manager of the Hotel Reforma) organized a Caravan of Good Will from Mexico City to Atlantic City in June 1938.[16] Using the slogan

"See America First, Start in Romantic Mexico," a group of 22 hotel owners and managers from Monterrey, Puebla, and Mexico City teamed up with Mexican diplomats in the United States and with the AMA, the Department of Tourism, the Pan-American Union, and National Railways of Mexico to combat the negative press about Mexico. Pérez reported that by meeting with American journalists, hoteliers, travel agents, and even governors along the tour route and in Atlantic City, their Caravan of Good Will succeeded in erasing misunderstandings about and destroying prejudices against Mexico.

Although the rates of tourist entry improved by late 1938, they still remained below those of 1937. Moreover, although both oil companies rescinded their false claims about the lurking dangers south of the Rio Grande, tourist promoters learned that they needed to be more active in publicizing Mexico. Both the oil nationalization and the hurricane incident illustrated the speed with which defamatory gossip about Mexico spread throughout the United States. It also reflected the residual broad and profound distrust of Mexico. Understandably, potential tourists, journalists, and politicians contemplated the contradiction between Mexico's recent oil nationalization and its efforts to promote mutual understanding and goodwill with its northern neighbor. Moreover, Mexico's leaders held steadfast to neutrality regarding the war in Europe, and even welcomed controversial figures such as Leon Trotsky to Mexico.

Yet by late 1938, in anticipation of a long and dreadful war in Europe, Mexico's tourist promoters, with President Cárdenas's blessing, seized an opportunity left open by a market entirely cut off by war— they made plans to establish the Mexican Tourist Association (AMT). How the AMT emerged is striking because it involved the same members of the revolutionary elite who, since 1928, had advocated the development of tourism and who had built a network of supporters throughout Mexico and the United States, including men like Luis Montes de Oca and Aarón Sáenz Garza. The first step in organizing the association came by way of a meeting between William H. Furlong, members of the Mexican Hotel Association, National Chamber of Hotels, National Railways of Mexico, and the AMA out of which they created a "Mexico Relations Committee" with Texas hotel associations in 1938.[17] The goal of the committee was twofold: to promote convention tourism to Texas and, from those conventions, to organize postconvention trips to Mexico. At one such convention held in Galveston, Texas in late September 1938 for hoteliers in the United States,[18] the Texas Hotel Association organized a postconvention tour to Mexico City. By personal invitation, President Cárdenas welcomed some 150 hoteliers to Chapultepec Castle for a dinner. Other invited guests included members of the revolutionary elite like former president Pascual Ortíz Rubio, Finance Minister Eduardo Suárez, Bank of Mexico Director Luis Montes de Oca, Foreign Affairs Minister Eduardo Hay, and Interior Minister Ramón Beteta. They also included financiers like National City Bank of New York President William B. Richardson, Mexican Mortgage Association President Alfonso Cerrillo, and 19 other guests who represented nearly all the banking and lending institutions in Mexico City.[19] Out of this brilliant organizing maneuver, in which an exchange of hotel knowledge took place, emerged the Mexican Tourist Association (AMT). The mastermind behind this event, Luis Montes de Oca, credited its success to the cooperation between Mexico and Texas. Under a private, umbrella organization, he hoped to bring together all private and government-related interests in tourism.

Unlike its ineffectual, government-organized predecessors that equally brought together government institutions and private enterprise but that hardly succeeded in motivating investments in publicity campaigns, the AMT formed and would remain under the direction of the private sector whose members were now, more than ever, ready to publicize Mexico's tourist industry. As a nonprofit, social service organization, the AMT was in a position to receive private and public donations that members could invest in tourist promotion. In cooperation with the government, the AMT established goals to complement the work of the National Tourism Commission and the Department of Tourism. It also received patronage from state ministries such as the Interior, Foreign Affairs, National Economy, Communications, and Finance as well as the Mexico City government (Departamento del Distrito Federal). From the private sector, AMT founding member institutions included the Bank of Mexico, National Railways of Mexico (FFCCN), Petróleos Mexicanos (Pemex), AMA, National Chamber of Hotels, Mexicana Airlines, Mexican Railways, South-Pacific Railways of Mexico, Missouri-Pacific Railways, travel agencies and, of course, Luis Montes de Oca. At its inaugural assembly held in February 1939, those present included men with long-standing ties to the early development and promotion of tourism. Men like Aarón Sáenz Garza, José Rivera R., Salvador J. Romero (FFCCN), Oreste Cabutti, Rafael Mondrágon (Mexican Railways), Luis Osio y Torres Rivas, Federico Miranda (Missouri Pacific Railways), W.L. Morrison (Mexicana Airlines, a subsidiary of Pan American Airways), Francisco Lona (FFCCN), and Leando Valdés (FFCCN) had all been active in tourism since the 1930s and even before.[20] Representatives from

FFCCN, for example, had prior experience handling publicity campaigns in the United States. As early as 1935, National Railways spent about Mex$676,000 on promotional materials and earned approximately Mex$22 billion in return.[21] Moreover, as members of the government-organized, Comité Nacional de Turismo (CTNT), they commissioned several studies on the benefits and strategies of tourist promotion. In 1937, Orozco Escobosa, of the railways publicity department, submitted to the committee a preliminary study on how much each sector of the private enterprise should invest in publicity. Based on statistics of tourist spending in Canada, Orozco concluded that Mexico could make more profit from motor tourists than those who traveled by railway. On average, motorists spent more money on lodging and food, unlike railway passengers whose meals and lodging were partially included in a train fare. He estimated that restaurants and hotels in addition to oil companies, commerce, nightclubs, theaters, and the FFCCN, should invest in tourist promotion.[22]

Likewise, Francisco Lona, longtime employee of National Railways who worked as its representative in Chicago in the late 1920s and continued in the public relations department throughout the 1930s to 1940s, submitted a study on publicity strategies to the CTNT in 1938. This study sought advice from R.J. Newton, a convention organizer from San Antonio who was working on a "Greeters Guide to Mexico." Among other things, he suggested a full-fledged publicity campaign. For free advertising, Newton suggested that tourist promoters invite important guests—movie stars, dignitaries, governors, and mayors—to participate in all-expense-paid tours of Mexico. Not only could organizers take photographs of their important guests at historic sites and mail them to the U.S. press, but they could also bet that their guests, who had a positive experience in Mexico, would spread positive press through conversation upon their return. Finally, Newton suggested that they frequently send out press releases to American newspapers to inform readers on the latest tourist news from Mexico.[23] Lona clearly adopted some of Newton's suggestions when he outlined the AMT's goals for 1939. In his plan, he suggested that the AMT send tourist posters as well as short films to the United States. He also made clear in the Public Relations section that the AMT should arrange trips for journalists and important U.S. figures in hopes that they, upon their return, would spread good news about Mexico.[24]

The earliest AMT reports from July 1939 that included a list of donations received and projects carried out, demonstrate the impressive breadth of their operation. Having received Mex$173,000 in donations since March of its first year, the AMT spent Mex$148,000 on advertising. Among the largest contributors were the FFCCN, Pemex, Bank of Mexico, DDF, Chambers of Commerce, Mexicana Airlines, beer, wine, and liquor companies, and owners of Mexico City cabarets and nightclubs.[25] In their end-of-the-year report, the AMT reported receipts of Mex$207,000 in donations and an expected Mex$665,000 in 1940. In part, the AMT expected an increase in contributions from a fundraising campaign that began under the direction of José Rivera R. and Ernesto J. Canales (Interior Ministry). As incentive to donators, the AMT promised to publish their names in a special monthly bulletin in which they would formerly recognize them for their patriotic contributions to tourism.[26] Mexico City hotels like the Hotel Ritz, Geneve, Guardiola, Reforma, Imperial, María Cristina, and Carleton as well as restaurants like Sanborn's, Manolo, and Lady Baltimore contributed.[27] Based on the steady influx of donations throughout its first year, these enterprises and the federal government recognized that with Europe now engaged in a war, Mexico could emerge as the natural leader of the new inter-American travel movement just beginning. Because war elsewhere meant that Mexico could build on peace and prosperity at home, donations from the federal government by the summer 1940 enabled the AMT to flood the United States with tourist publicity.

In its first year, the AMT was prolific in publicizing tourism to Mexico. During its first six months, it distributed throughout the United States 60,000 copies of a brochure on train travel via Missouri Pacific Railways entitled, "Sunshine over the Border"; Missouri Pacific Railways received 20,000 copies, the AMT received 10,000, and FFCCN distributed the other 30,000 to their offices in Mexico City, Chicago, New York, Los Angeles, El Paso, New Orleans, and San Antonio.[28] In this brochure, David S. Oakes wrote the text for Missouri Pacific Railways and took readers through a description of what they would see in Mexico while on the "Sunshine Special," its sleeper train from St. Louis to Mexico City. According to Oakes, once passengers passed through Monterrey, they entered "real Mexico." The "real Mexico" (or central Mexico), he wrote, should be the destination of all passengers who wished to truly understand their neighbors.[29] In addition to brochures, the AMT also produced and distributed throughout the United States 10,000 posters destined for the walls of train stations, Mexican Consulates, and hotels in Texas and in Mexico.[30] Produced by the AMT in conjunction with the Department of Tourism, these posters included images of Pátzcuaro with the slogan "Overnight from Mexico City" as well as images of Oaxaca, an aerial view of Taxco, and several that referred to Mexico in general. The AMT sent some of these posters to Hollywood in another publicity campaign a few years later with which fledgling starlets posed. Some of these posters included its most famous one simply entitled, "Visit Mexico," with an image of the *china poblana* and the *charro* (see chapter 3, note 10), her male counterpart, while another advertised train travel to Mexico stating, "Handy . . . Mysterious, Colorful . . . Mexico," accompanied by the image of a train passing through a hand in which was drawn picturesque Mexico.[31]

In addition to working with Mexican organizations, the AMT also cooperated with American ones to produce useful brochures that advertised a variety of vacations from postconvention to motor travel, most of which were written in English by American authors. For example, they published and disseminated 5,000 postconvention brochures, 160,000 copies of "Sunshine over the Border," and 100,000 copies of the brochure "Mexican Highways" with help from the Texas Hotel Association, the AMA, the Department of Tourism, and railway companies. In addition, the Ministry of Communications and Public Works (SCOP) and Mexico's national lottery helped to produce 400,000 copies of regional brochures divided equally among Tasco, Cuernavaca, Oaxaca, and Morelia-Pátzcuaro-Urupan, a small portion of which were written for a Mexican audience.[32] In addition, they produced and distributed 100,000 copies of the brochure entitled "Mexico—The Faraway Land Nearby," written by Howard Phillips for the AMT. This luxurious 48-page guidebook introduced readers to Mexico with a colorful cover showing a typical, rural woman of indigenous descent sitting in front of a *nopal* cactus (see figure 4.1). Behind her was the dome of a colonial church and blue sky on the horizon. With nearly 50 black-and-white photographs accompanied by descriptions, this brochure was designed to familiarize readers with Mexican culture, its traditional holidays, arts and crafts, and gastronomy. Phillips also provided information on motor, railway, steamship, and airline travel as well as requisites for border entry and customs. He dedicated close to half the guidebook to descriptions of Mexico's attractions and featured the capital city (in six pages) as the center of all interstate motor travel to outlying cities and towns such as Tepoztlán, Cuernavaca, Cuatla, Taxco, Acapulco, Puebla, Tlaxcala, and Huejotzingo (each described in 1–2 paragraphs). Finally, the brochure provided readers with two spectacular foldout maps. The first, a strikingly colorful "Descriptive Map of Mexico," illustrated transportation from the United States to Mexico and

Figure 4.1 Jorge González Camarena, woman on cover of "Mexico—The Faraway Land Nearby," Howard Phillips for the Mexican Tourist Association, 1939.

within Mexico. And the other, "A Map of the heart of Mexico City," illustrated the city's finest hotels and important buildings such as the U.S. Embassy, Palace of Fine Arts, National Library, and National Cathedral.

The AMT also forged relationships with U.S. publicity agents, making use of American advertising know-how to make their organization known throughout the United States. In 1939, the AMT entered into a temporary agreement with a New York firm, The Hamilton Wright Organization Inc., who offered its services free of charge for six months with the hope of winning the AMT and the Mexican government as clients. In so doing, they produced 150,000 free lines of favorable publicity for Mexico's tourist industry.[33] Respected for its campaigns on behalf of the Italian and Egyptian governments and for the city of Miami, Florida, Hamilton Wright received a short-term contract with the AMT in 1940. The timing for this partnership could not have been more opportune as rumors spread in June 1940 about a brewing revolution in Mexico and President Cárdenas's alleged sympathies toward fascists and communists. Journalist Betty Kirk, employee of Hamilton Wright, swiftly wrote an article to counter these rumors. The agency distributed her article to no less than one hundred U.S. newspapers. In her article, Kirk described the president's sweeping moves against "subversive" activity when he expelled the German Embassy's press attaché, Herr Arthur Dietrich, and closed the Nazi-subsidized magazine, *Timón*.[34] Finally, the AMT paid the Caples Company, an advertising firm with offices in New York, Chicago, Los Angeles, and Omaha,[35] a total of US$13,000 from October 1939 to December 1939 for the distribution of 24,600 lines of positive news to over 19 newspapers in 14 U.S. cities. Some of these newspapers included the *Chicago Tribune, Detroit Free Press, Atlanta Constitution, Kansas Star, St. Louis Globe Democrat* and *Cleveland Plain Dealer*.[36]

Finally, the AMT carried out an intense pro-Mexico campaign using radio and film developed by their longtime employee, William H. Furlong. In any given year, Furlong gave at least 35 presentations. In his repertoire, he showed a color film loaned to the AMT by Missouri-Pacific Railways entitled, "Mexico," as well as another produced in 1937 by the Pan-American Union entitled, "Rollin' Down to Mexico." Moreover, his good friend C.G. Renier, program director of KMOX "The Voice of St. Louis," organized radio shows such as the 1939 program FIESTA to which invited persons spoke on the wonders of Mexico.[37] Moreover, the radio station broadcasting from the St. Anthony Hotel in San Antonio ran 20-minute spots featuring traditional Mexican music and song. Radio became central to the diffusion of information about Mexican culture and about travel. In July 1939, for example, with large contributions made by the FFCCN, the AMT sponsored a broadcast of the Mexican Symphony Orchestra over the waves of XEW, the radio station owned by Emilio Azcárraga. Under the orchestral leadership of conductor Carlos Chávez, this program was dedicated to the growing friendship between Mexico and the United States, and it featured guest announcers Lucas de Palacio and Judge Alvin R. Allison, named by Texas Governor W. Lee O'Daniel as that state's "Ambassador of Goodwill" to Mexico.[38] A few months later, the FFCCN inaugurated the radio program, "Mexico for Travel, Mexico at the Fair," on several radio stations in New York City with financial cooperation from General Electric, American Express, and the United States Travel Bureau.[39] Finally, in 1941, National Railways representative in San Antonio, Francisco Alatorre, helped organize and fund a radio program entitled, "Know Your Neighbor," with sponsorship from the Institute for Latin American Studies (ILAS) at the University of Texas at Austin. Beginning on July 7, 1941, ILAS transmitted twenty-four radio programs, each fifteen minutes in length, which offered listeners traditional Mexican music and informative lectures on government and society.[40]

With all its activities, the AMT easily demonstrated to its members and patrons that advertising was the key to the making of a successful tourist industry, especially in light of world events.[41] With an administrative council that reflected some of the nation's most prominent individuals,[42] it should come as no surprise that the AMT played a vital role in attracting approximately 130,000 U.S. tourists to Mexico. By fall 1939, donations to the AMT's publicity campaigns increased. For example, FFCCN donated an additional Mex$100,000, the Finance Ministry gave Mex$200,000, and Pemex Mex$100,000.[43] In an effort to further mobilize capital, the AMT kept its members informed by distributing a bimonthly bulletin that consistently emphasized the need for and benefits of publicity in the United States. The reports reminded readers that the tourist markets to Europe and Asia were cut off for years to come. One AMT bulletin reported that a favorable 1939 article published in *Better Homes and Gardens* elicited no less than nine hundred inquiries for tourist information and brochures about Mexico to the Chicago office of National Railways.[44] Another report provided members with excerpts from American newspapers that suggested Mexico as the beneficiary of the European war because tourists would inevitably look south for their future vacations.[45]

By summer 1940, the AMT had convinced tourist interests from both the official and private sectors that the war in Europe had opened a world of opportunity in which Mexico would undoubtedly profit. Despite the onslaught of another tourist crisis following Pearl Harbor and U.S. entry into World War II, the AMT and other tourist promoters used the media and advertising to transform their nation into a good neighbor during the war years.

"WE ARE READY": PUBLICIZING GOOD NEIGHBORLINESS IN THE UNITED STATES

In unison, Mexico's tourist promoters from the government's Department of Tourism to the AMT shouted: "Yes, We Are Ready!" Indeed by 1940, Mexico proved its eagerness to welcome U.S. tourists. It had paved highways and roads connecting the United States to Mexico, as well as those connecting Mexico City to tourist attractions in outlying towns and cities. It offered new accommodations along its highways and even some luxurious first-class hotels, restaurants, and nightclubs in the capital. Above all, Mexico enjoyed a period of relative peace, stability, and democracy, an atmosphere in which tourists felt increasingly familiar and increasingly comfortable. To kick off his final year as president, Cárdenas officially codified into law, the years 1940 and 1941 "A Tourist Biennial."[46] On the one hand, his proclamation formally expressed Mexico's goodwill toward the United States. His declaration intentionally echoed FDR's push for U.S. travel throughout the Americas as the ideal medium to foster mutual understanding and friendship, especially in light of the international crisis. On the other hand, Cárdenas used fashionable language to evoke goodwill, calling his administration and the Mexican people "friends of peace and of American brotherhood."[47] Under the aegis of goodwill, his proclamation sought to promote Mexico's tourist industry. Unlike FDR's declaration that urged U.S. citizens to participate in inter-American travel, Cárdenas's declaration represented a "call to arms" aimed at creating a united front between government ministries, state and local governments, and private enterprise that would aid in making Mexico the perfect host to thousands of expected guests. Even though this united front had been in the making for several years and seemed to coalesce around the Mexican Tourist Association by 1939, Cárdenas used the proclamation to make public his administration's dedication to this endeavor. Moreover, the president made clear that Mexico was ready to be the principal recipient of the new inter-American travel movement for two reasons. First, Mexico City had been selected by the Pan-American Union to host the Second Inter-American Travel Congress (IATC) on September 15–24, 1941. Second, Mexico was a geographically desirable ("in the center of the hemisphere") destination increasingly known for its tradition of warm hospitality.[48]

Cárdenas's "Tourist Biennial" marked a pivotal turning point in the history of Mexico's tourist industry. It made public an important vision held by the United States, namely that Mexico, more than any other Latin American nation, would play a central role in spurring hemispheric and democratic solidarity. To be chosen as host of the Second Inter-American Travel Congress, after the first was held in San Francisco in 1939, meant that the Pan-American Union, and the United States in general, saw Mexico as a leader in Latin America. Furthermore, U.S. officials recognized that Mexico City had the facilities to house, feed, transport, and entertain representatives from the 20 invited countries—the United States, Cuba, Dominican Republic, Guatemala, Honduras, El Salvador, Costa Rica, Nicaragua, Panama, Colombia, Venezuela, Ecuador, Chile, Bolivia, Paraguay, Brazil, Argentina, Uruguay, and Peru. It also must have demonstrated a political integrity and proven democratic spirit to be host for such a prestigious meeting to which the United States sent some of its most prominent representatives, namely Bruce Macnamee of the State Department's United States Travel Bureau.[49] U.S. officials hand-picked Mexico as the greatest beneficiary of this new inter-American travel movement by choosing it to play host to a congress expressly designed to provide the know-how to help Latin American governments develop their own tourist industries so that they, too, might attract U.S. tourists. In so doing, the declaration made official the belief that Mexico was prepared for visitors. Mexico's government responded with a seven-page layout in its official magazine, *Migración, Población, Turismo*, under the title, "Yes! *We Are Ready!*"[50] According to this photo essay, Mexico offered U.S. tourists good paved roads, modern hotels, fine colonial buildings, archaeological delights, "wild virgin nature," and "above all . . . *hospitality!*"[51]

The "Tourist Biennial" also marked a pivotal shift in the promotion of Mexico's tourist industry. It not only gave a boost to earlier publicity campaigns coming out of Mexico but it also gave rise to a new ideological tool, goodwill, with which to promote tourism. Because the "Tourist Biennial" proclamation made explicit Mexico's plan to cooperate with the United States as "American brothers," wrote President Cárdenas, AMT publicity campaigns noticeably began to use (and invariably overuse) the concept of Mexico-U.S. solidarity and good neighborliness to promote tourism. With both U.S. recognition and the president's declaration of cooperation, the AMT began to couch tourism to Mexico as a way to fulfill the greater purpose of spreading democracy and goodwill. And they did so with the blessing and encouragement of government officials who, beginning in early summer 1940, assigned treasury monies to the AMT for the purpose of publicizing Mexico in the United States. Since this declaration in January 1940, President Cárdenas appeared increasingly supportive of the tourist industry. In fact, following oil nationalization in 1938, he saw the value in improved U.S.-Mexico relations especially because the U.S. government began to look for defensive and diplomatic alliances in Mexico, and Latin America in general.

It should come as no surprise that Cárdenas, like other tourist promoters, saw a golden opportunity for Mexico to prosper during this time of war. Through publicity like the "Tourist Biennial" declaration, he worked to undo the damage caused by oil nationalization and his "open door" policy in which Mexico became a refuge for controversial figures like Leon Trotsky. By late spring 1940, as Cárdenas prepared to leave and Manuel Ávila Camacho prepared to enter office, rumors of possible revolution spread throughout the U.S. press to which the president openly responded with assurances of stability. In a statement sent to the press, the president chided those who spread malicious propaganda about Mexico and emphasized his nation's cooperation with the United States, recognizing that war in Europe placed the United States and Mexico into a new friendship. Further, he reassured readers that "Americans may visit Mexico without fears of any kind. They will always find our hand outstretched in friendliness to greet them."[52]

Less than a month after this press release, President Cárdenas held a special meeting in Puebla with AMT members Francisco C. Lona of National Railways and J.J. March of Pemex in which they requested federal monies for the AMT's summer publicity campaign to combat negative propaganda about Mexico that, they argued, had been spread once again by U.S. oil companies. Accompanied by Francisco Trejo (head of the Department of Tourism and General Office of Population—part of the Interior Ministry—and president of the government's National Tourism Commission) and Ernesto J. Canales (Interior Ministry and AMT patron), the five men met for forty minutes and easily convinced the president to budget US$10,000 for the AMT campaign in June in addition to the Mex$200,000 contribution that the Finance Ministry had already set aside for the AMT.[53] This unprecedented donation reflected the first genuine economic cooperation between private enterprise (AMT) and the government for the promotion of tourism.

Almost immediately, the AMT put the money to use. Lucas de Palacio, AMT manager, sent a press release to travel agents throughout Mexico to reassure them that the AMT and government was doing everything necessary to increase tourist rates that had slightly declined after the recent rumors about possible revolution. In the press release, Palacio included excerpts from the June 11 *New York Times* article that reported a meeting between U.S. and Mexican Secretaries of State Sumner Welles and Ramón Beteta. This, the journalist argued, demonstrated improved relations between neighbors, especially now that the European war had thrown the two closer together.[54] Palacio announced to travel agents that federal monies in the amount of US$10,000 had been donated to the AMT for use in publicizing Mexico in the United States, part of which had been used to pay the Hamilton Wright agency for an intense campaign in June and July. Finally, he attached to the press release the first of many pro-Mexico articles to be distributed by the company, in which Betty Kirk told readers that President Cárdenas cleaned Mexico of Nazis and Communists and that he called for hemispheric solidarity against totalitarianism.[55]

By 1941, the relationship between the government and the AMT grew stronger as did U.S.-Mexico relations. Two important factors that explain this should not be underestimated: first, business-minded Miguel Alemán was Interior Minister and, as such, head of the Department of Tourism. Under Alemán's leadership, the federal government more readily donated to the AMT, giving, for example, a total of Mex$127,000 for its fall 1941 publicity campaigns.[56] Second, Mexico's reputation was successfully being reinvented during this era of goodwill. In a speech to the Los Angeles Publicity Club, for example, historian Osgood Hardy of Occidental College referred to what was happening between the United States and Latin America as the rise of a "new Pan-Americanism."[57] On the occasion of the fiftieth anniversary of the Pan-American Union, Dr. Osgood argued that the Good Neighbor Policy and war in Europe gave rise to this new sense of Pan-Americanism based on the need to create a moral union in the Western Hemisphere. By 1941, Mexicans increasingly used to their advantage this cooperative atmosphere caused by war. Their government and the AMT were finally in a position to embark together on the greatest spectacle of goodwill: the 1941 "Presidential Tour."

Though its name may be misleading, this tour was designed to lure presidents of U.S. motor clubs and travel agencies, not political leaders, to the "real" Mexico that lie beyond its border towns. The AMT and the Department of Tourism organized this two-week "Presidential Tour" from March 30 to April 13 as a way to draw attention to and create publicity for the upcoming Inter-American Travel Congress to be held in Mexico City from April 14 to April 19. Moreover, as one contemporary journalist pointed out, it served to foster friendship between two democratic nations as well as to convince participants that Mexico was "an ideal vacationland."[58] With funding from the Mexican government and the AMT, and in cooperation with the Mexican Automobile Association, Pemex, FFCCN, Mexican Hotel Association, and others, a 19-car caravan comprised of U.S. and Mexican delegates as well as journalists from *Time*, *Fortune*, *Life*, *Christian Science Monitor*, and various newspapers set off on April 1 from San Antonio to Mexico after an opening ceremony at which Alejandro Buelna, Jr. (head of the official Department of Tourism) welcomed the U.S. delegates to Mexico on behalf of President Ávila Camacho.

For two weeks, Mexico's representatives dazzled the U.S. delegation.[59] The Texas Highway Patrol escorted the caravan from San Antonio to the border at which time Mexican Highway Patrol guided it all the way to Monterrey. On the outskirts of Monterrey, the local Chamber of Commerce welcomed the party on the road to the Hotel Monterrey. After a luncheon, the caravan drove to Valles where Tamaulipas Governor Magdaleno Aguilar met delegates on their brief stop in Ciudad Victoria. On their way from Valles to Mexico City, they ate lunch at Ixmiquilpan while entertained by a live mariachi band. They stopped once more to see the *Monumento de Buena Amistad* (Monument of Good Friendship), built in 1936 by the American Colony in Mexico City, located along the Pan-American Highway just on the outskirts of the capital city. At the gates of Mexico City, beside the *Indios Verdes* statue, Interior Ministry officials greeted the party on behalf of Governor Javier Rojo Gómez.[60] Officials escorted delegates to a reception at the Hotel Reforma and then to their rooms at the Hotel Geneve, Hotel Reforma, Hotel Ritz, and Washington Apartments. The "Presidential Tour" was pure spectacle. When delegates arrived by train to Fortín de las Flores, Veracruz, for example, a town famous for its gardenias and orchids, one hundred schoolchildren with bouquets of local flowers greeted the delegates as they disembarked. Veracruz Governor Lic. Jorge Cordan and his staff met the delegates as they arrived at Antonio Ruiz Galindo's recently opened ultra-resort, Hotel "Ruiz Galindo."[61] That evening, Ruiz Galindo, revolutionary capitalist par excellence, organized a "Tropical Festival," held by the hotel's pool on top of which 2,000 gardenias floated. Behind the governor's table was a sign that read "Welcome," which was surrounded by both the Mexican and U.S. flags made entirely of flowers. Broadcast over the radio were speeches given by the governor, the *Christian Science Monitor* representative, Efraín Buenrostro of Pemex and the AMT, and Lic. Horacio Casasus of the AMA. Delegates enjoyed traditional Mexican music played by Veracruz's official, 18-piece orchestra (*la Orquestra Típica*), a Marimba band, and a dance orchestra from Orizaba, Veracruz. Finally, friends, wives, and girlfriends of the local hosts dressed in regional costumes to give their guests a sense of colorful and diverse Mexico.[62]

Mexico's government officials and private entrepreneurs went to great lengths to please some 49 invited guests from the United States whose departure conveniently coincided with the arrival of U.S. and Latin American delegates about to take part in the most prestigious tourist conference held in the Americas. The "Presidential Tour" served to transform Mexico's image from the unruly to good neighbor in an effort to attract U.S. tourists to Mexico. In a farewell telegram to U.S. delegates as they passed through Monterrey on their way back to San Antonio, General Enrique Estrada (vice-president of the AMT and manager of the FFCCN) reiterated these goals of Inter-American solidarity and travel:

> Visits such as [this] of the Presidential Group serve the cause of Inter-American solidarity . . . since your honest interpretation of Mexico will bring about [an] interchange [of] spiritual values between our peoples through intensified large-scale travel.[63]

If it were not for Pearl Harbor and U.S. entrance into World War II, then the "Presidential Tour" would have had more immediate results. Although 1941 was Mexico's best tourist year, World War II stymied but did not altogether destroy rising numbers. Instead, Mexico seemed destined to benefit from the incredible postwar tourist boom on account of well-planned publicity campaigns carried out during this era of goodwill. Even when tourist rates dropped by half after the United States entered into war, inter-American travel by U.S. tourists remained central to projects of the Pan-American Union, Organization of American States and office of later-American Affairs throughout the 1940s and into the Cold War of the 1950s.

Despite their losses during World War II, the AMT prepared for the expected postwar boom. In one AMT press release to U.S. travel agents, Lucas de Palacio poignantly wrote, "Debacle elsewhere has brought about an unprecedented solidarity between the United States and Mexico."[64] After Mexico declared war on Axis powers in May 1942, the common war effort brought the two countries even closer together as the U.S. economy increasingly relied on Mexico for wartime goods and contract (*bracero*) labor. With keen publicity sense, the AMT in the fall of 1942 sent a press release to the United States entitled, "Vacationing with a purpose."[65] No longer just a good neighbor, Mexico was now an ally who understood wartime conditions. The AMT aimed this tourist advertisement at middle-class Americans such as the typical foreman at a defense plant (Johnny Adams) and female stenographer (Janice Meredith) who had earned their vacation time and were looking for an economical vacation with fun and sun. According to this advertisement, Mexico was not only the logical answer because it suited any budget—clerical workers like Janice or her rich boss—but it also helped Janice and Johnny keep inflation down because their money was spent in Mexico.

*   *   *

Ordinary Americans may have agreed that it was "patriotic to vacation in Mexico," as this advertisement exclaimed, because tourist rates remained surprisingly steady between the years 1942 and 1945, although they never surpassed the industry's best year in 1941. Nevertheless, over the next few years, the AMT sent reassuring words to their members in an effort to keep morale high. By mid-1942, the AMT faced the reality that rubber and oil rations in the United States presented severe obstacles to what they had hoped to be a boom in tourism. Unlike other crises, this one was about potential financial losses. Whereas tourists spent an estimated Mex\$55 million in Mexico in 1941, in the first six months after the attack on Pearl Harbor they spent a mere Mex\$14 million.[66] By the end of 1943, the AMT had advertised relentlessly. It distributed throughout the United States a total of 714,000 publications in the form of posters, brochures, maps, and hotel directories. In so doing, Mexico not only remade its image abroad but also paved the way for a postwar tourist boom.

CHAPTER 5

PYRAMIDS BY DAY, MARTINIS BY NIGHT: SELLING A HOLIDAY IN MEXICO

According to the authors of the 1954 travel guide, *Mexico and Cuba on Your Own*, tourists in Mexico City could visit pyramids during the day, drink martinis at night, and "embark on a whirl of nightclub fun and dancing which only the most modern metropolis could offer."[1] Still today, the sale of a holiday in Mexico's capital city relies on its embodiment of both modernity and antiquity. This combination has proved to be one of the most successful selling points for the nation's tourist industry. Only recently, the Ministry of Tourism (SECTUR) advertised to tourists their nation's "many moods": its ancient (pyramids and colonial treasures) and cultured (ballet, opera, museums, and nightlife) sides.[2] Current travel essays featuring Mexico City continue to package it as a "land of contrasts," where tourists find "centuries of history plus cell phones." Finally, contemporary travel writers still compare Mexico City to the world's most sophisticated cities like Paris, New York, and London, but argue for its uniqueness found in nearby pre-Columbian ruins.[3]

By 1939, Mexico's revolutionary elite, many of whom were tourist promoters, packaged and sold Mexico City to U.S. tourists as a city undergoing great change. Descriptions and slogans such as a city "of one hundred disguises" or a "new-old city," have been a mainstay since the industry's formative years. Each conveys an image of a city that now bears five centuries of history on which trends and traditions are inscribed. Whereas travel writers today refer to a decline in crime rates and a decrease in pollution as evidence for Mexico City's continued move toward modernity, those from the 1940s looked to its blossoming cosmopolitanism. Specifically, they defined transitions underway in the capital on popular notions of pleasure such as luxurious hotels, swanky nightclubs, smart entertainment, leisure and exquisite cuisine that, only years earlier, tourists were hard pressed to find. In so doing, they carved a unique niche for tourism to Mexico City unrivaled by its greatest competitors Cuba and Canada and by other Mexican destinations. By 1940, the capital embodied the best of all worlds because it contained vestiges of the past and increasingly offered comforts of the present. Vacationers in Mexico City engaged not only in urban tourism, but also in healthy and educational excursions reminiscent of nineteenth-century Grand Tours and romantic tourism to Niagara Falls. In only a few hours from the bustle of the capital, tourists visited the pyramids, sulfur baths and spas, vast beaches, and Indian villages.[4] As one contemporary observer poignantly wrote in an article entitled "Motor Sparks," the capital was no longer a final destination but the principal point from which tourists ventured on short day, weekend, or weekly trips, and to which they usually returned.[5] Mexico City became the starting point for many national roads and highways that led to potential tourist sites. From Mexico City, for example, motorists could journey on highways and roads to Cuernavaca, Acapulco, Oaxaca, Veracruz, Teotihuacan, the Desert of the Lions, Tepotzotlán, and Cuatla.

However, inside the package labeled Mexican vacation, tourists had always found antiquity but not modernity. Folklorist and travel writer Frances Toor, for example, emphasized in her 1936 and 1938 guides to Mexico that tourists should not expect to find much in the way of entertainment in Mexico City.[6] She warned pleasure seekers that amusements in the capital were not only wholesome but also limited. And among the sparse nightspots in the capital, few had "floor shows."[7] By the postwar tourist boom in 1946, after close to two decades of tourist development and promotion, her description of Mexico City dramatically changed. In her *New Guide* she compared the capital to other cosmopolitan cities and assured tourists that they would never be bored.[8] Mexico City nightlife, she wrote, offered pleasure seekers an experience comparable to New York's smartest cabarets and swankiest supper clubs. Clubs like Ciro's, El Minuit, and El Patio offered audiences toe-tapping live orchestras and fantastic floor shows.

The swiftness with which Mexico City seemed to emerge as a cosmopolitan tourist delight is striking, reflecting the transformative power and maturation of Mexico's tourist industry. Relative peace and stability in Mexico after 1929 made the development of a tourist industry possible. The president's declaration that Mexico intended to enter the race for the tourist dollar in 1929 made tourism an official government project. Emerging government and private tourist associations between 1929 and 1935, who studied and supported the industry, had developed the infrastructure to support tourists' demands for easy travel and comfortable accommodations. The inauguration of the Nuevo Laredo-Mexico City Highway in summer 1936, which linked the United States to central Mexico, made the capital city accessible. And on the eve of World War II, tourist promoters used to their advantage goodwill to publicize Mexico as a "Good Neighbor" and, in turn, made their nation acceptable in the American tourist imagination. Inherent in such advances was the way in which elite tourist promoters packaged, marketed, and sold an image of their nation. At the same time that they launched publicity campaigns to reshape Mexico's image, they also created a language and iconography that equated the nation's capital with the past, present, and future.

Alex Saragoza has briefly mapped a shift in the packaging of Mexico as a tourist destination from folkloric imagery set against a local backdrop to folkloric imagery set amidst modernity by the 1940s. He argues that this move away from depicting an essentialist past and move toward creating an image of Mexico as a potpourri of past and present served to define national identity.[9] Likewise, Eric Zolov suggests that this conflation of old and new or the "cosmopolitan-folklórico" discourse prevalent in tourist imagery from the 1940s to 1960s, successfully attracted American tourists who willingly consumed this package of Mexico. As this chapter suggests, the reinvention of Mexican traditions can specifically be found in the way that tourist promoters packaged and sold Mexico City as the conglomeration of antiquity and modernity by the early 1940s. Consequently, the capital city emerged changed and eventually afflicted by this dual image, attesting to the transforming power inherent in tourist development.

Reinventing Traditions: *La Indígena* and Other Regional Types[10]

After years of development, travel writers by 1939 were able to sell a dynamic Mexican vacation to potential U.S. tourists. Between the years 1936 and 1939, members of Mexico's tourist organizations worked diligently to ensure that motorists found accommodations along the new international highway. Under the leadership of Luis Montes de Oca, leading banking institutions offered credit to investors willing to construct hotels in Mexico City, along the highway and at likely tourist stops.[11] After oil nationalization in 1938 caused tourist rates to drop sharply, tourist pioneers quickly turned the industry around when they embarked on publicity campaigns through the U.S. mass media. As the Mexican Tourist Association (AMT) flooded the press with slogans about Mexico's goodwill toward the United States, officials from the north and from the Pan-American Union helped Mexico's cause by encouraging tourism to Latin America as an expression of democracy and freedom.[12] Increasing U.S. reliance on Mexico during the war years, as an ally and as a source of raw materials, gave Mexico an edge over competing destinations. With new confidence, tourist promoters had the tools with which to attract American tourists to Mexico. In tourist literature produced in Mexico and the United States, travel writers began to brag about Mexico's many modern attractions: a well-developed highway and road network whose web spun from Mexico City; well-organized tourist services run by members of the AMT; newly constructed or renovated first-class hotels; and a pulsating nightlife (cabarets and supper clubs) for the smart set in Mexico City. Through imagery such as this, promoters attempted to attract tourists. By 1939, for example, pictures of Mexican women dressed in regional costumes graced the covers of tourist guidebooks, travel posters, and magazine advertisements. While her regional identity varied—she may have been from Veracruz, Puebla, or Tehuantepec—her dark skin personified Mexico's indigenous past and her welcoming smile personified Mexican hospitality. Drawn to reflect both sensuality and strength, she mirrored broader changes underway in Mexico.

As the landscape of Mexico City was transformed by tourist development throughout the late 1930s and early 1940s, tourist promoters modernized the woman who personified Mexican hospitality. They increasingly juxtaposed traditional regional types with symbols of a nation in the making, a nation on the rise. Whereas she personified Mexico's tradition of hospitality, background images of fancy hotels, paved highways, and urban architecture symbolized Mexico's advances. In certain pictorials on Mexico City tourism by the mid-1940s, she enjoyed a complete makeover and reflected sheer urban cosmopolitanism in fashion, refinement, and charm.

By 1939, the Mexican Tourist Association mass-produced the image of Mexico as a traditional indigenous woman dressed in a regional costume to attract American tourists. Adorning the cover of the colorful and lengthy tourist brochure entitled, "Mexico—The Faraway Land Nearby," written by Howard Phillips, the AMT distributed well over 100,000 copies of this brochure in the United States (see figure 4.1).[13] Underneath the title that simply reads "MEXICO," the smiling woman meant to personify the nation turns her head away from the artist as if she is watching something beyond the viewer's scope. With a pleased, excited, and even flattered expression on her face, she gently rests one hand on her throat and leans sideways with the other on a rock. She is dressed in a full, white muslin skirt with a pink stripe and an embroidered top. With dark hair pulled back, her head is covered with a long, striped *rebozo* (shawl) that is pulled just behind her ear to show that she wears a large gold-hoop earring. Her face is full, only barely painted with blush and lipstick, and she exemplifies health. To her right is a blossoming *nopal* (prickly pear) cactus with fruit; in the far rear is the dome of a simple colonial building. And above her is a blue sky with low puffy clouds.

Drawn by artist Jorge González Camarena, this image, with its soft colors and rounded shapes, conveys a sense of Mexico's uniqueness and its friendliness. The earth tones of her moderately dark skin embodied in a woman of Indian, and perhaps Spanish, descent evokes feelings of warmth and genuineness that tourists could expect to find during a holiday in Mexico. The viewer is unsure at what or at whom she is smiling that seems to provoke her expression of flattery and modest surprise; but at what she is watching—an event or a passerby—provokes the viewer's sense of curiosity. And because she is more pleased than surprised, she reassures the viewer that she or he could not expect to be taken completely aback by what they might find as a vacationer in Mexico. Finally, the landscape denotes an eternal spring with a flowering cactus and blue sky. Together, the symbols of *lo mexicano* in this image take shape: the *nopal* cactus represents the Mexica-Aztec past, the orange-red domed building represents the colonial past, and the friendly *indígena* (indigenous woman) represents the optimistic present.

The text in "The Faraway Land Nearby" confirms what the woman named Mexico is meant to personify. She embodies change, progress, and optimism, not innocence or domination by the north; in other words, she was meant to personify modern Mexico.[14] Phillips writes that by highway, railway, sea, and air, tourists arrive to find the making of a modern nation. He attributes this to revolutionary reconstruction,[15] suggesting that tourists see this new society—its massive road building and irrigation projects and its rural peoples who are learning to read and write. He also encourages tourists to witness the

changing face of Mexico City with its building boom, where slums
have given way to high-rise apartments, and where suburbia is being
made. With little to no unemployment, he wrote, tourists could see
firsthand that Mexico, embodied by the woman on the cover, was an
advanced nation.

In 1940, the government replicated the image of Mexico as the
hospitable woman in the concluding part of a six-page tourist advertisement in their magazine *Migración, Población, Turismo* (Migration,
Population, Tourism).[16] This time the woman who symbolizes
Mexico came from the beaches of Veracruz. Because it was published
in black and white, one notices the contrasts of color: her cotton off-
the-shoulder blouse is stark white as are her teeth, the flecks of ribbon
in her hair, the sky, and the sand on the beach; meanwhile her eyes,
hair, skin, and lips are dark as are the palm trees in the background.
Turning from the artist and looking behind her bared shoulder, she
uses both hands to hold up to her ear a large conch shell. Standing
with a pleasant smile and a healthy glow on a beach with palm trees
and a clear sky, she lures tourists with sights and sounds of the sea.
Although she appears more sensual than her earlier counterpart, she
equally personified the same hospitality tourists could find in a
Mexican holiday. And as part of a larger series of photographs that
comprised the layout entitled, "Yes, *We Are Ready!*" she is one of the
more traditional qualities that Mexico had to offer. For example, the
first image in this layout was a photograph of the Mexico-Laredo
Highway that showed viewers its safety features, namely paved surface
and guardrails. The next page featured a photograph of the towering
Hotel Reforma in Mexico City between images of things to see and
do in the capital city such as the Desert of the Lions and the historic
center (*Zócalo*). In contrast to the modern Hotel Reforma, the essay
included a photograph of Teotihuacan, with men standing clad in
Mexica-Aztec costumes, as well as a serene photograph of the volcano, Iztaccíhuatl, taken from the canals of Xochimilco. At the con-
clusion of the layout, the text reads, "hospitality," placed above and
below the image of the *veracruzana* (woman from Veracruz) on the
beach listening to the conch shell.[17] As enduring as Mexico's many
regional types, and as enduring as its beautiful women, so Mexican
hospitality remained a mainstay of modernity and antiquity that
tourists were bound to find.

By World War II, the imagery of the woman who personified
Mexico in tourist advertisements began to reflect a new strength and
productivity. Because, as advertisements explained, "debacle elsewhere meant peace between two previously contentious neighbors,"

tourist promoters flooded the United States with messages about goodwill in an effort to encourage patriotic vacationing to Mexico.[18] To holiday in Mexico, as one AMT advertisement declared, helped ordinary Americans cement democratic ties to the south. The necessary rest enjoyed in Mexico by wartime managers, secretaries, and factory workers further ensured increased productivity upon one's return to the workplace as well as kept inflation down because, by spending money in Mexico, fewer demands for everyday products were placed on the U.S. domestic market.[19] In this wartime context, two images distributed by the government's Tourist Department stand out for their bold use of the *mestiza*, or the woman of mixed Indian and Spanish descent.

In 1942, the Tourist Department, with help from Galas de México S.A., a printing company known for its production of popular calendars, produced and distributed throughout the United States 30,000 copies of a poster entitled, "*Visit* MEXICO"[20] (see figure 5.1). Rendered from an original photograph, well-known Mexican artists painted said image onto canvas. That painting was then photographed again for use on calendars and posters.[21] In this image, painter Jorge González Camarena reinvented the traditional *indígena*, replacing her with the new *mestiza*, meant to signify strength, health, wealth, and productivity. Unlike his earlier depiction of the traditional indigenous woman, he discarded the softly brushed, round contours, and warm colors used earlier, for the use of vivid colors, sharp edges, straight lines, and symmetry in an effort to convey a sense of realism. Moreover, unlike the images of regional women so far described, this new buxom, *mestiza* beauty (this time she appears a combination of Mexica-Aztec, *china poblana*, *veracruzana*, and Anglo) gazes directly at the artist and the viewer. Standing upright, precisely in the forefront of a thriving tropical forest rich with fruits, wildlife, and vegetation, the woman with a broad smile appeared totally confident and self-assured. She also exudes health, strength, and productivity as she effortlessly held a heaping bowl pineapple, papaya, bananas, oranges, guava, lime, and guayaba. Unlike other tourist images, her low-cut, short-sleeved top embossed with a Mexica-Aztec face along the neckline is taut over her full breasts through which her nipples show. Finally, her hair, in two braids, rest between her bosom, and she wears a headband of white flowers, two oversized gold-hoop earrings and a choker of red and black beads around her neck.

At first glance, the personification of Mexico in this tourist poster seems entirely sexual. Indeed, it is hard to deny the sensuality she is meant to convey. But in the context of wartime relations between the

Figure 5.1 Jorge González Camarena, Woman on poster of "Visit Mexico," Mexican Tourist Association and Department of Tourism, 1942. Library of Congress, Prints and Photograph Division [reproduction number, LC-USZC4-4357].

United States and Mexico, a more complex meaning emerges. Rather than mere sexuality, the woman who symbolizes Mexico conveys a renewed strength and confidence to potential tourists. No longer does she look away seductively; instead, she stares straight at her intended audience. She boldly invites tourists to experience Mexico's progress and to witness its productivity. Moreover, her embodiment of various types—the modern *mestiza*, colonial *china poblana*, and prehispanic Mexica-Aztec—surrounded by symbols of Mexico's fruits of labor reflects the fusion of the nation's past, present, and future. In a much different way than before, this personification of Mexico represents a nation in the making during World War II and a nation at terms with its history.[22] Finally, this image of Mexico as the inviting but strong *mestiza* woman is undeniably anglicized. That is, while her skin is dark, her features are remarkably non-Indian with high cheek bones and softened nose. This depiction suggests the way in which the artist, González Camarena, produced an image of the ideal Mexican woman that was palatable for tourist consumption and familiar to ordinary Americans. Despite the artist's dedication to the nationalist cause of revolutionary reconstruction, as professed by his son in conversation with the author,[23] the woman on the "*Visit* MEXICO" poster served to sell the elite, tourist agenda by simultaneously designing an image of the ideal Mexican woman who signifies modern Mexico and an image of what tourists expected—that of the sensuous, exotic yet familiar Mexican woman.[24]

Another poster that shows the transformation from indigenous to *mestiza* and the symbiosis of exotic and familiar is the wartime poster produced by the AMT and the government's Department of Tourism in 1944 (see figure 5.2). Here, the modern *mestiza* transforms into a symbol of power and ingenuity. With a subtitle that reads, "For the SAME Victory! MEXICO," artist Francisco Eppens designed the personification of Mexico as a woman to be bold, even fierce, with dark skin, bare breasts, strong abdominal muscles, and powerful arms.[25] As if on the move toward a common enemy, the woman in this tourist poster raises her arms above her head, her hands in fists. Although she does not directly face the audience because she is moving toward something, her eyes are intensely fixed and her mouth opened as if straining. In other words, she appears prepared to fight. This warlike readiness is only made clearer because the figure of the woman overpowers the background of Mexico's landscape in which a train passes through pointy, green hills peppered with simple structures. Together, the images convey activity and movement. The train is captured in motion with a lingering cloud of steam pouring from its

Figure 5.2 Francisco Eppens, Woman on poster of "For the SAME Victory! MEXICO," Mexican Tourist Association and Department of Tourism, 1944. Library of Congress, Prints and Photographs Division [reproduction number, LC-USZC4-4357].

engine. She, too, moves with her hair in mid-air and the white sheet that covers her lower body curved, both lifted by a strong wind created by her own force. Even more than the 1942 poster of the woman holding fruit, the woman who personifies Mexico in this 1944 tourist poster conveyed that nation's confidence like never before. Though her strength and form appear superhuman, Mexico, as engendered by this woman, was indeed powerful by the close of World War II. Through this image and poster, prospective U.S. tourists understood Mexico's firm commitment to democratic ideals and good neighborliness. Indeed, the nation had begun to prove its dedication to democracy by 1940 when Cárdenas cracked down on suspected fascists and Nazis in Mexico, and continued to do so when, in late 1942, President Ávila Camacho declared war against Germany and Italy, and sent Squadron 201 to fight in the Philippines. Of the many factors underlying Mexico's united efforts with the United States after 1939 was tourism. The personification of Mexico as this superwoman conveyed to the American public that it was a fierce partner in the fight for democracy. Finally, the moving train, a long-standing symbol of progress and modernity, suggests that Mexico was also an ideal host to tourists.

From *La Mestiza* to Mexico City

Like the conflated images of the traditional regional type and the modern *mestiza* meant to personify both the tradition and progress of the Mexican nation, tourist promoters and travel writers advertised tourism to Mexico by focusing on depictions of the familiar and cosmopolitan capital city. Seen in photographs of a light-skinned and highly fashionable Mexican woman and visitor, or in the urban architecture and cityscape, images of cosmopolitanism embodied a modern sensibility that tourists could expect to find in the capital. As the modern urban woman, she is seen buying flowers at the market, eating ice cream at the lake, and sipping a cocktail with her date at a nightclub. In so doing, promoters demonstrated the many tourism possibilities during a holiday in Mexico. Still more, these images reflected familiarity. Whereas images of the *mestiza* and regional types used to personify the Mexican nation evoked some sense of exoticism and difference, those used to advertise Mexico City consistently compared the capital to other well-known U.S. and European cities such as New York, London, or Paris. Whether depicted as a woman or a building, tourist promoters and travel writers used these images to sell Mexican modernity.

The sale of modern Mexico was not before possible as earlier literature can attest. Essays and pamphlets published by Mexico's tourist organizations from the late 1920s and early 1930s packaged a trip to Mexico not as a modern vacation, but as an inexpensive, romantic and, more importantly, educational experience. Still, even before the highway linking Texas to Mexico City was complete, tourist promoters argued that the best place to begin a holiday or student excursion was the nation's capital. In a 1929 advertisement for the Summer School of the National University published by the Bank of Mexico, its author lured potential students to Mexico City by focusing on the vestiges of history found in and around the capital, which would only enhance one's learning experience.[26] Likewise, archaeologist Manuel Gamio lectured readers on the larger "transcendental" meaning behind a holiday in Mexico.[27] More than a bargain vacation where the tourist dollar would go far, he argued, tourists in Mexico could experience the process of evolution and witness the rise of modern civilization. For those interested in anthropology, ethnology, and archaeology, the recently excavated pyramids illustrated the living and breathing world of centuries ago. One 1929 Bank of Mexico tourist pamphlet gave readers a list of the things to do in Mexico City, emphasizing the treasures of the Mexica-Aztec era, colonial period, and nineteenth century. The author of the pamphlet encouraged tourists to begin in the historic center. After visiting the National Palace and National Cathedral, tourists should see prehispanic art housed at the National Museum, the Academy of San Carlos, and the House of Tiles. Then it suggested that tourists take a rented car or a hired chauffeur along the Paseo de la Reforma, perhaps stopping first at the Alameda Central, toward their final destination, Chapultepec Park and Castle. For those who desired to see more recent architecture, the author invited tourists to visit the Bank of Mexico and to pass by the Ministry of Foreign Affairs, Ministry of Communications and Public Works (SCOP), Post Office, Ministry of Education, Public Health Department, and the National School of Teachers. Finally, the author suggested itineraries for day and weekly trips around Mexico City. By streetcar or automobile, tourists could visit Xochimilco, la Basílica de la Virgen de Guadalupe, San Ángel, Coyoacán, and Churubusco. And by bus and automobile, tourists could take excursions to Tlalpan, Texcoco, Tacuba, Tepoztlán, Teotihuacán, Puebla, Cuernavaca, and Pachuca.[28]

Likewise, two years after the world-renowned travel agency Wagons Lits-Cook opened its doors in Mexico City in summer 1929, they began to offer tourists a selection of short and extended guided tours that departed from the capital. Each included transportation, lunch, and an English-speaking guide who lectured on the historical and archaeological. Everyday but Tuesday, the agency offered trips in and around the capital or trips to outlying towns such as Puebla, Cholula, and Cuernavaca. At the cost of Mex$12, tourists enjoyed a full-day tour through the city (7.5 hours in length). Included on the itinerary were visits to the capital's historical monuments and buildings: the National Pawn Shop (1775), Metropolitan Sagrario (1749), National Palace (1693) and Cathedral (1667), Preparatory School in the San Ildefonso Monastery (1749), Vizcainas Convent (1732), La Merced Monastery (1616), the National Theatre (Palacio de Bellas Artes), Chapultepec Castle and Park, and the city's newest residential suburb, Chapultepec Heights. The guided tour also stopped to eat traditional food at a Mexican restaurant and visited a brewery where they sampled Mexican beer.[29] For the same price, Wagons Lits-Cook offered a more rugged trip to the floating gardens of Xochimilco that included stops at the Guadalupe Shrine, Indian market, Tenayuca Pyramid, the Pedregal, and Colonia Hipódromo. The group also visited the mummies housed at the Carmen Church in San Ángel and took a canoe ride on the canals in Xochimilco. Finally, on Thursdays and Sundays, Wagons Lits-Cook gave a guided tour of the pyramids at Teotihuacan and Acolman Monastery, returning at 3 p.m. on Sundays to take the group to a bullfight.

These early travel pamphlets and itineraries certainly demonstrate that tourists had things to do and see while on vacation in Mexico City, but early figures on tourist rates indicate that the capital received only a small percentage of visitors before the international highway was complete in the summer of 1936. Still more, tourist groups from both the private and public sector knew that Mexico City lacked modern accommodations and diversions deemed important by pleasure-seeking U.S. tourists who chose to vacation in Mexico. As Frances Toor pointed out in her 1938 guidebook, tourists would expect to enjoy their day excursions but not night entertainment. Tourists, she suggested, wanted more from their evenings than a picture show. By 1940, boring nights in Mexico City were a thing of the past as the capital was visibly transformed. Its population had more than tripled between the years 1930 and 1940, from 520,000 to 1.8 million residents. Hotel construction alone transformed the city landscape. For example, in 1935, Mexico City had a total of 22 officially registered hotels (registered with the city government) with 1,596 rooms.[30] In less than 7 years, by early 1942, the number of registered hotels in the capital jumped to 55 with a total of 3,582 rooms.[31] Together the government's Department of Tourism and the Mexican Tourist Association began to compile hotel listings for directories to distribute throughout the United States. Despite the drop in tourist rates following Pearl Harbor, tourism groups were still optimistic, and, in 1942, they distributed 20,000 hotel directories.[32] Hotel construction during World War II continued with great fervor in expectation of a postwar boom. In 1944, for example, figures show that an additional 1,500 rooms were under construction in Mexico City.[33] By 1946, 11 new hotels were being built to provide an additional 4,420 rooms to accommodate the burgeoning tourist industry.[34]

One of the most important publications to capture in words and imagery the dramatic changes under way in the capital city was the magazine *Pemex Travel Club*, produced by the government's official gasoline and oil company, Petróleos Mexicanos (Pemex). First published in 1939 under the direction of J.J. March and with contributions from American writers and journalists living in Mexico,[35] this English-language tourist magazine created a new language that refashioned the earlier packaging of a Mexican vacation as simply romantic and ancient. In fact, this publication helped create an iconography of the cosmopolitan city. Distribution figures suggest that the *Pemex Travel Club* reached a wide U.S. audience. In 1942, it sent out 600,000 copies to United States, free of charge, to interested individuals who joined the club by mail.[36] And despite record-low tourist entries during wartime, Pemex distributed 395,000 copies to members in 1945.[37] The *Pemex Travel Club* featured articles about Mexico City and other outlying attractions. It also offered detailed information on the costs of motor travel, updates on highway conditions, news on recent advancements in gasoline and oil products and services, tips on the Spanish language, and information about Mexican culture and customs including dates of important national and regional holidays. Writers assisted tourist promoters with their broader publicity campaign to make Mexico an acceptable vacation spot. They worked to dispel prevalent rumors and, instead, spread good news about Mexico's partnership with the United States. Contributing writer, Victoria Marshall, for example, wrote an article entitled, "Mexico Likes America," in which she encouraged her fellow citizens not to believe rumors that Mexicans showed their hatred toward Americans by throwing stones at their automobiles.[38] And, in nearly every issue, writers reported news that illustrated improved U.S.-Mexico relations.

As a publication owned by Mexico's newest state-run oil company, its principal goal was to attract U.S. motor tourists to the heart of

Mexico. To do so, March featured essays about and images of modern Mexico City. March repeatedly used photographs of fashionable, cosmopolitan women to personify modernity in an effort to make the capital desirable and familiar to tourists. One cover from August 1940, for example, featured a photograph of the new urban woman (see figure 5.3).[39] Choosing a large bouquet of flowers at a local market, the light-skinned, fashionable model smiles at the bouquet she selects. In contrast, the flower vendor is indigenous, quite possibly a rural migrant, who is hard at work. Whereas the vendor has a long dark braid down her back and is wearing a typical market apron, the modern woman has shoulder-length dark curly hair and is dressed elegantly in a white suit, black blouse, and smart black and white hat that subtly tie the colors together.

If this 1940 magazine cover conveyed to readers the idea that the average urban woman had fashion sense, not to mention leisure time, then its accompanying feature essay on Mexico City told readers what she, an urbanite, might do for fun. Entitled, "Mexico City After Dark," this article featured images of an audience of snappy dressers in eveningwear—tuxedos and gowns—attentively enjoying a floorshow at an undisclosed nightclub.[40] In the accompanying story, the writer suggested a few hotspots popular among locals and tourists alike that fit any budget. For a more formal atmosphere, where prominent U.S. tourists, wealthy European immigrants, and local elites gathered, the author urged readers to experience the Tap Room located in the Hotel Reforma, as well as El Patio, Manolo's, and Alt Heidelberg. For a more provocative night out, especially for single men, the author suggested that tourists visit Waikiki but warned against "slumming" without a local guide. The thrill for tourists, the author concluded, was the urban experience with a "truly foreign flavor." In other words, like the cosmopolitan woman, Mexico City was that perfect combination of familiarity and exoticism.

In another issue of the *Pemex Travel Club*, the cosmopolitan city was personified by images and text of a day in the life of the smart set—young women and men from Mexico City and from abroad who spent their leisure time cavorting around the capital. Entitled, "Life in Mexico," after the nineteenth-century journal kept by Fanny Calderón de la Barca, this four-page layout begins with a photograph of the city skyline from a spot above the Paseo de la Reforma.[41] Although the image captured few tall buildings, the caption emphasized its "roof-top gardens" featured at many of its new buildings and hotels. Together with the paved and tree-lined avenue this image conveyed Mexico City's "sights of modernity" that tourists could expect

Figure 5.3 Urban woman on cover of *Pemex Travel Club*, Vol. II: 113-A (August 1940). Courtesy of Hemeroteca Nacional.

to find. The photographs featured fashionable Mexicans, an American summer student mingling with locals, and popular venues where everyone spent their leisure time. For example, one photograph showed a young woman who, according to the caption, visited Mexico City to take classes at the National University's Summer School. She and her Mexican beau reflected true "Good Neighborliness" as they enjoy a picnic together at Chapultepec Park on a sunny afternoon. The next few images introduced readers to the Mexico City's "smart set." In one photograph, two couples in formal attire descend from a staircase on their way out for the evening. In another, a fashionable cosmopolitan woman in a fine suit, her hair in an updo accentuated by gold lamé pillbox hat, purchases silver at a local curio shop. For evening activities, the final images introduced readers to Mexico City nightlife. Beginning with another photograph of the same woman from the curio shop who now dined at a plush nightclub, it showed her sipping cocktails with friends. The interior of the swanky nightclub where they is set against walls padded with a rich silk or velvet fabric and a crystal chandelier hangs over the table. Another photograph features a young couple sipping cocktails at a bar. Here, an elegant and fair young woman with a flower in her hair sits on a bar stool and enjoys conversation with an attractive suitor. On the other side of the young woman is another fair-skinned, blonde also sitting at the bar engaged in conversation with a caption that read, "Mexican Night Clubs are becoming famous the world over."

Prospective tourists learned from these images that Mexico City was cosmopolitan with its modern buildings, thriving nightlife, and glamorous urbanites. The models featured in these photographs all engaged in leisure-time activities such as shopping, eating, and drinking. These signifiers of modernity used by travel writers and tourist promoters to sell a holiday in Mexico that began in the capital were magnified by the text that accompanied the photographs from "Life in Mexico." Using the description of the day in the life of a female American tourist, the writer gave readers a closer glimpse into the social world of Mexico City. The story begins with a woman waking up in her hotel room in Mexico City. Readers learned that after she breakfasted at Sanborn's,[42] she then drove to the pyramids with friends to contemplate antiquity. Such reflection on the past made the American tourist a bit solemn, so she lunched at a popular French restaurant where she spotted the Minister of Foreign Affairs Ezequiel Padilla and Mexican film star, Mapy Cortes. Later, after changing into her best clothes, she headed to the horse races at the Hipódromo de las Americas, a racetrack owned by Bruno Pagliai and inaugurated with great pomp on March 6, 1943.[43] At the racetrack she spotted, among others, chic Mexico City socialite Adela de Obregón Santacilia wearing a fur hat and scarf ensemble. Upon returning to her hotel room, she changed once again to prepare for her night out, choosing a semiformal sequined suit and hat, rather than an evening gown. She and her friends first sipped cocktails and danced at a nightclub with a French atmosphere, then they continued on to a supper club for exquisite food and music, finally ending their evening at a "plebeian club for the rousing floorshow." What did she have in store for the next day, the author asked? Of course, once she returned to Mexico City after spending the day in Cuernavaca, she had tickets to the Mexican Symphony Orchestra.

Readers may have doubted their own abilities to handle so much diversion in a single day during their vacation, but the writer set out to overwhelm readers with the many things to do in Mexico City. Its many references to cosmopolitan fare available to tourists, coupled with images of people and places that personified the modern capital, focused readers' attention on the familiar, namely on things one might find in any modern city especially Hollywood. In this essay, modernity overshadowed antiquity so much so that pyramids were mentioned only in passing; and, when mentioned, they seemed to evoke depression in the fictional American tourist. To shake off this feeling, the tourist dined at a fancy and fashionable French restaurant. In so doing, she was reminded that Mexico City justifiably enjoyed a reputation as the "Paris of the New World." Yet unlike its faraway counterparts in Europe and Asia, *Pemex Travel Club* readers learned that the capital city had distance, dollars, and diversity on its side. Without traveling thousands of miles, impossible during World War II anyway, and without spending hundreds of dollars, American tourists got more for their money and time south of the border. In just one nearby country, tourists found attractions comparable to those found in Egypt, London, Paris, and Hollywood. Packaged as such, travel writers increasingly compared Mexico City to other first-world cities. In so doing, they made the capital more familiar and less exotic.

In "Mexico City-Modern Version," readers learned that the capital was no longer a land unknown.[44] Instead, its photographs featured aspects of urbanity that tourists could find elsewhere. The text, for example, included a photograph of an intersection described as one of the city's busiest street corners. The caption assured readers that the image they saw in the photograph—a traffic light and "streamlined" building—was in fact taken in Mexico City not Manhattan. Above this image readers saw a photograph of a typical scene found along the

Paseo de la Reforma: a tall statue set against the backdrop of an even taller building. This time the caption reminded readers that they should not mistake this photograph for one taken in Barcelona because it, too, was taken in Mexico City. This visual comparison between Mexico's capital and other European, U.S. and Asian cities continued relentlessly with a photograph of the Central Post Office that the writer compared to the Italian city of Florence, of an ordinary plaza thought to be reminiscent of Berne, Switzerland, and of a busy street in the capital's "Chinatown" that might remind tourists of Beijing.

While *Pemex Travel Club* used these images to make Mexico City familiar in the tourist imagination, the text emphatically emphasized its uniqueness. Not only was the capital easy to reach from any major U.S. city, but also the rate of exchange between dollar and peso fit almost any tourist's budget. Still more, the writer suggested that tourists could witness the dramatic changes underway in the capital where sophistication gradually replaced provincialism, where modern buildings emerged alongside colonial ones, and where native life coexisted with modern life, namely nightlife. According to this and other essays, these contrasts of modernity and antiquity epitomized the lure of Mexico.

Finally, in an essay entitled, "Mexico of a Hundred Disguises," cosmopolitan capital was likened to a fashionable and beautiful woman. The author suggested that like all charming women with their many faces and moods, tourists could find aspects of other international cities in Mexico's capital.[45] The author compared Mexico City to a charming hostess who was able to converse with and appeal to all her guests. Behind her many disguises, the capital looked like Paris, Vienna, Toledo, and even Stockholm. Tourists could find the mood of Buenos Aires in its skyscrapers, shops, and parks along Juárez Avenue. They would be reminded of Beverly Hills when they drove through Mexico City's new residential suburb, Lomas de Chapultepec, where large modern homes have been built on spacious green lawns. Moreover, this essay featured photographs of these and other striking sites that reflected its many disguises such as the pointed arches and tiled façade of an apartment building shown to remind readers of La Alhambra in Granada, Spain.

Essays in the *Pemex Travel Club* portrayed Mexico City as modern by comparing it to popular tourist destinations in Europe that were increasingly inaccessible during World War II. Travel writers and tourist promoters fashioned a holiday in Mexico City as a twentieth-century version of the Grand Tour. By featuring modern subjects in its

photographs—urban men and women, diversions and architecture—
and by relentlessly comparing them to familiar points of reference in
other major cities, the essays in the *Pemex Travel Club* struck a chord
with prospective U.S. tourists in search of an inexpensive, urban,
somewhat exotic but comfortable vacation. By the early 1940s,
Mexico's cosmopolitan capital not only met their requirements but
also like a charming hostess, seemed to conform, at least in theory, to
tourists' every desire.

DOMESTIC TOURISM

Whereas travel at home and abroad had characterized American culture since the Grand Tours to Europe, it was not as prevalent a concept in Mexican culture where the majority of the population was
rural. With the exception of Mexican elites who vacationed abroad
and at home, a Mexican middle class capable of mass travel only
began to emerge by the 1940s. For most who survived on the edges
of the formal economy it was nearly impossible to travel or take a
"vacation," so that only some workers, mostly government employees, were receptive to the promotion of national tourism. Given
these obstacles, tourist organizations only halfheartedly invested
their money and time promoting national tourism. In their 1940
prospective budget, for example, the Mexican Tourist Association
(AMT) set aside Mex$137,000 for publications aimed at U.S.
tourists, and only Mex$10,000 for publications aimed at national
tourists.[46] In 1939, whereas the AMT published 765,000 English-
language tourist publications destined for the United States, they
produced a mere 60,000 in Spanish to remain in Mexico.[47] Among
these, the AMT published 10,000 copies of a brochure on automobile caravans and 50,000 copies on train travel entitled "Viajes de
vacciones."[48] The AMT also distributed 5,000 copies of an educational brochure in 1939 entitled, "Turismo—más dinero para
Usted," designed not only to encourage businesses to continue their
investment in tourism but also to create a "tourist consciousness"
among local businessmen.[49]

Promotional literature aside, efforts to foment national tourism
emerged as early as 1936 and increasingly after 1938. When the U.S.
government established the United States Travel Bureau many
Mexicans believed it posed a threat to the growth of their tourist
industry. Although founded in part to promote U.S. travel abroad, this
bureau focused much of its energy on promoting travel to and within
the United States, which meant that it hoped to keep U.S. tourists at

home.[50] Part of the larger inter-American travel movement, this bureau departed from the goals of the Pan-American Union and, instead, encouraged Americans to get to know their own country. This, coupled with the plunge in the number of visitors following oil nationalization in 1938 and the prospect of world war in 1940, gave tourist promoters every reason to turn to the underdeveloped national market and encourage Mexicans to get to know their country. *Ejidatarios* (or communal landholders) of Villa Úrsulo Galván organized one of the first excursions for Mexicans. In 1936, the government circulated an advertisement to all federal employees encouraging them to participate in a ten-day tour and stay at the Hotel and Spa "Barra de Chachalcas."[51] Meant to benefit the campesinos in Veracruz, government employees were given the opportunity to enjoy an excursion to the countryside where they rode horses to thermal baths, and where they could hunt and fish. Employees paid in five, bimonthly installments at the total cost of Mex$80 per person. The following year, the AMA-Guadalajara Club organized a series of three-day automobile excursions for its 128 members in 1938. They visited Autlán, Jalisco, and neighboring Michoacán. By 1939, the AMT in cooperation with the Mexican Automobile Association and Petróleos Mexicanos organized the first 50-car caravan that drove from Mexico City to Cuernavaca; participants spent the night at the Hotel Chula Vista.[52]

In an effort to encourage Mexicans to take part in national tourism, the government began to regulate vacation time. In 1937, for example, Article 12 of the labor code for employees of credit institutions instituted that those with good service records receive guaranteed vacation time: those workers with 1–10 years of service at a single institution earned 20 vacation days; those with 10–15 years earned 25 days; and those with more than 15 years earned 30 days. Moreover, the law obligated employees to take their paid vacation.[53] By 1941, when Mexico welcomed a record-breaking number of tourists, the AMT and Department of Tourism sought to reform labor laws for federal employees to guarantee them restful vacations. Rather than one vacation in December, this new law proposed two vacation cycles: from November 21 to November 30 and from December 11 to December 20. This, they argued, not only ensured more productive workers but also encouraged national tourism because Mexicans would not face obstacles when trying to relax at potentially crowded vacation spots during high tourist season.[54]

When foreign tourist entries to Mexico plunged in 1942, the AMT introduced the concept of tourism as a leisure-time activity in its national tourist campaign. The association placed advertisements in

Novedades and other newspapers, and broadcast announcements on radio stations XEW and XEQ[55] It also circulated an announcement to hoteliers, restaurateurs, and other tourism-related business people in May 1942 requesting that they consider lowering their daily rates to accommodate the budget of most national tourists.[56] According to the announcement, the situation was grim because U.S. entry into World War II provoked a sharp drop in foreign tourism. With a standard of living in Mexico well below that of its neighbors, national tourists could not pay for luxurious accommodations. The AMT suggested that rather than suffer extraordinary profit losses, hotels and restaurants should work to accommodate the more limited budget of most Mexican tourists.

Finally, while canvassing in Acapulco (of all places) in 1945 during his campaign for the presidency, Miguel Alemán echoed the importance of reducing accommodation costs so that Mexicans could get to know their own country. He called national tourism a patriotic act. The hotelier, he argued, helped foster national unity and morale by enabling ordinary Mexicans to travel throughout the republic as tourists. Among other things, the time spent relaxing strengthened Mexico's economy through improved worker productivity upon returning to the workplace.[57]

The AMT's publicity campaigns during World War II aimed at promoting domestic tourism but never proved especially successful in the larger scheme of the tourist industry during the period considered in this study. As only a temporary solution during wartime conditions, upon closer examination one finds that ordinary Mexicans, whether employees with guaranteed paid vacations or not, found other forms of recreation and relaxation. Many, rather than take the train or drive to Cuernavaca, Taxco, and Acapulco, enjoyed their vacations at home. By the mid-1940s, a spirited nightlife had emerged and Mexicans, as much as U.S. tourists, sought pleasure in the evening. What developers constructed to meet the entertainment needs of pleasure-seeking American tourists and to demonstrate the cosmopolitan character of the capital city (the martinis that complemented the pyramids), found its way into the everyday lives of ordinary and not-so-ordinary Mexicans. As a result, Mexico City's nightlife symbolized the urban modernity so central to the packaging of a holiday in Mexico.

WHAT WAS A REAL HOLIDAY IN MEXICO?

By 1946, efforts by travel writers and tourist promoters to package and sell a Mexican holiday as the convergence of modernity, found in

Mexico City, and antiquity, found in nearby pyramids and colonial treasures, came to a head when MGM released its travel brochure musical, *Holiday in Mexico*. Although the musical was meant to take place in the capital, Mexico rarely makes an appearance. In fact, it is unlikely that MGM filmed on location and one can be sure that not a single actor in the cast was from Mexico. Nevertheless, these oversights, typical of Hollywood's "Golden Age," did not seem to pose a problem for American audiences who were clearly delighted by what they saw. *Holiday in Mexico* grossed US$3.7 million and was one of Hollywood's most loved musicals at the time. Whereas Hollywood producers notoriously cast Portuguese-born Carmen Miranda as a generic brand of Latin American, the directors of *Holiday in Mexico* cast Spaniards with amazing musical talents as Mexican. Spanish-born violinist, and big-band leader, Xavier Cugat, the man who made the rumba, cha-cha-cha and tango commonplace the world over, starred as the wacky Mexican musician with his talking Chihuahua[58] and full orchestra. Cugat's intentionally bad Mexican accent, his music, his dog, and his orchestra were meant to add a wild, if not stereotypical, Latin American flavor as well as some comic relief to the film. Meanwhile, famous and refined Spanish pianist, José Iturbi, stood out as the symbol of high Mexican culture and became the target for young Powell's misguided affections. Unlike loud Cugat and his jealous, dark-skinned girlfriend, Iturbi was presented as a grandfather figure, a talented classical musician, and worldly Mexican who tried and failed to teach his maid to prepare scrambled eggs. Finally, the gringo characters, and thus stars of the musical, included Walter Pidgeon as the U.S. Ambassador to Mexico and widowed father to his jealous and overbearing daughter, singing sensation Jane Powell. To add even more internationalism to the film, MGM cast Budapest-born singer Ilona Massey as the ambassador's love interest.

The thin story line centered on Powell who was organizing the entertainment for a party her father had planned for a group of dignitaries living in Mexico. Brazen and coy, she used the son of the British ambassador, who happened to be in love with her, to drive her around the capital so that she might hire Mexico City's finest musical arrangements, namely Massey, Cugat and his orchestra, and Iturbi. To do so, Powell interrupted Cugat and Massey as they rehearsed for the evening floorshow at his nightclub, and she interrupted Iturbi's rehearsal with a chorus of beautiful women as they geared up for a theater performance to take place in a few weeks. Refusing to take no for an answer, Powell used her charm to convince all to perform at her father's party. In the process, she managed to get "mixed up" with

Iturbi by mistaking his musical interests for love. Despite a few shots of the two youngsters in a convertible, the audience hardly sees Mexico City. Nearly the entire film was shot within the confines of a building or an estate: inside the Ambassador's home, inside Cugat's nightclub, inside Iturbi's living room, and, at the end of the film, inside a theater where Powell unabashedly performed "Ave Maria" with Iturbi. When audiences finally catch a glimpse of local capital-city life, they see inside the world of Cugat's nightclub. In this scene, Powell and her British pal, both dressed to the nines, sneak into Cugat's nightclub to spy on her father drinking cocktails with Massey. In so doing, U.S. audiences saw into the glamorous world of Mexico City nightlife where locals, tourists, and members of the international community swayed to pulsating Latin American rhythms and drank fancy cocktails in an altogether plush atmosphere.

What did U.S. audiences find so appealing about a *Holiday in Mexico*? In part, the answer can be found in Mexico's own sales campaigns. Whereas Mexico's image in tourist posters and guidebooks by the 1940s conveyed progress and a growing strength and confidence, promoters and travel writers marketed the nation's capital as familiar, as a place where tourists would find styles and diversions reminiscent of Hollywood and other urban, and to a lesser extent exotic, attractions far away. It should come as no surprise that while *Holiday in Mexico* failed to convey to audiences a broader sense of Mexico's uniqueness, it succeeded in creating for U.S. audiences an image of Mexico City as cultured, cosmopolitan, international, and, above all, exciting. Through the refined classical music of José Iturbi, the big-band Latin rhythms of Xavier Cugat, the sultry sound of Ilona Massey, and the wholesome voice of Jane Powell who performed at Mexico City nightclubs, parties, and theaters, audiences imagined their own holiday in Mexico, with just the right touch of high culture, sensuality, and spice. The production and release of *Holiday in Mexico* illustrated that by 1946 Mexico City was not only commonplace in the American tourist imagination but was also envisioned, even by Hollywood film makers, as a cosmopolitan capital city.

For many, this 1946 Hollywood musical portrayed the real Mexico. Although the film hides Mexico behind Spanish disguises, both Cugat and Iturbi are meant to personify a bourgeoning metropolis. In contrast to popular imagery of the Mexican bandit and revolutionary common in the United States throughout the early twentieth century,[59] these new depictions suggested a modern Mexico and cultured urbanites, both images tourist promoters were unable to convey before the 1940s. Seen in guidebooks as early as 1940, the capital's burgeoning nightlife was in fact uniquely Mexican, for it had emerged not only to satisfy pleasure-seeking American tourists but also to satisfy pleasure-seeking *chilangos* (people from Mexico City) and members of a growing international community. They, like their northern counterparts, equally demanded modern diversions and fashionable entertainment. The demand and popularity was so high that by the close of World War II, an entire nightlife movement emerged in Mexico City such that nightclubs became a space in which tourists, Mexicans, and resident European émigrés drank their martinis, swayed their hips, and tapped their feet to the same live orchestras.

* * *

This new Mexican grandeur, as chronicler and playwright Salvador Novo called it in his award-winning 1946 essay by the same title, was found in the capital's cosmopolitanism—its luxurious hotels and swanky nightlife.[60] Tourists and locals alike needed only to pick up Novo's essay or a copy of journalist Carlos Denegri's magazine *Noctámbulas* (Nightlife-ing) to keep up with the latest trends in Mexico City fun where bartenders poured martinis at the capital's finest nightspots including Ciro's, San Souci, Bottom's Up, El Patio, Bar 1-2-3, and Minuit. Moreover, while tourists flocked to Mexico City after the war to see antiquity at nearby pyramids and in colonial churches, they also came in search of refined and elegant pleasure south of the border. There, at a good price, they experienced the glamour of a first-world capital city in a unique setting.

Epilogue

During moments of consciousness, Artemio Cruz laid on his deathbed remembering the course of his life that took him from rags to riches, from loving young man to bitter adulterer, from patriotic revolutionary to ruthless capitalist. In one of his many flashbacks that constitute the narrative of Carlos Fuentes's novel *The Death of Artemio Cruz*, the author provides his reader with a snapshot of Mexico City in 1941 highlighting the process of change underway in his main character, the nation, and the revolution. The flashback, for example, follows Cruz's estranged daughter and wife who venture from the exclusive neighborhood of *Las Lomas de Chapultepec* to shop downtown. At a bridal shop where they are choosing her wedding gown, the saleswoman reminds herself of the American business adage "the customer is always right" as she struggles to deal with their indecisiveness and arrogance.[1] The flashback also takes us to the famous Sanborn's Restaurant where, over waffles and pound cake, mother and daughter debate the English pronunciation of actress Joan Crawford, agreeing on the incorrect version of "Cro-for."[2] After more shopping and a break over two Canada Dry orange sodas, mother and daughter are horrified by a vicious dog fight that takes place en route to their chauffeured car. Meanwhile, Artemio Cruz also arrives downtown for a meeting with American investors who are looking for a Mexican partner—more like a front man—in a mining venture. Upon his arrival, Cruz adjusts his suit in the reflection of an office window. At that exact moment, Fuentes writes, "a man identical" to Cruz does the same; this man also happens to wear the same suit and to have the "same nicotine-stained fingers."[3] But whereas Cruz heads for the elevator, the man heads off into the street. The flashback then takes us to Cruz's meeting with the Americans who offer him an investment opportunity. Rather than acquiesce to their offer, Cruz plays hardball by counter-offering that they pay him an extraordinary amount of money to guarantee a concession for their venture on Mexican soil. Thinking back on this episode, Cruz admits that he made a counter-offer to put the Americans in their place: "so they would let [him] in as their equal."[4] Although a wealthy and powerful businessman, he admits to having an inferiority complex that stems from being Mexican, from living in a disadvantaged society of ineptitude, dirt, and poverty as opposed to Americans who live in an advantaged one of utilitarianism, cleanliness, and wealth.[5]

In this one flashback, Fuentes comments on the kind of alienation that has emerged in Mexico City as a product of modernization. He alludes quite literally to the kind of "dog-eat-dog world" that the capital city has become as well as the process of Americanization that has begun to change Mexican business practice and Mexican culture. He echoes what Samuel Ramos and Octavio Paz wrote about years earlier,[6] namely that Mexicans deem themselves less worthy than their northern neighbors and as a result imitate that which they are not. Finally, Fuentes laments the failure of the Mexican Revolution, which in his view produced corrupt businessmen like Cruz and a society divided by nouveau riche and working class. In contrast to the "grandeur" of modernization described by Salvador Novo in 1946, Fuentes looks back on this same era as decadent and the process by which Mexico got there as callous.

Tourism played a role in the making of a modern Mexican society that increasingly came under fire by writers like Carlos Fuentes and José Emilio Pacheco, by filmmakers like Emilio "Indio" Fernandez and Luis Buñuel, and by social scientists like Oscar Lewis.[7] For them, the influx of American products, the rise of a consumer culture, and emerging industrialization came at a cost to traditional Mexican values such as family and to core values of the revolution such as sovereignty. While these and other works appraised the consequences of economic development, tourism remained an unrecognized cause of change in Mexico. Perhaps its subtle and seemingly benign nature has made it a subject that, until recently, scholars have overlooked. But as this work has shown, the development of tourism in Mexico contributed to national development in ways one might expect: it led to the emergence of a professionalized service industry and greater employment opportunities, to an advanced transportation infrastructure of highways and airports, to public health improvements like potable water and sewage systems, to an impressive array of hotels throughout the nation, and to new diversions like nightclubs. For these reasons, tourist developers associated with the government and the private sector in Mexico made tourism central to broader modernization projects of the 1930s and 1940s. But it also contributed to national development in less quantifiable ways. Tourism increasingly brought Mexicans and Americans into contact with each other, which functioned to close the gap of cultural misunderstanding and served to gain repeat customers and greater profits. Although some scholars have argued that these encounters have had little effect on Mexicans themselves,[8] when thought about critically the kind of interchange that takes place between affluent American tourists and an often struggling local population, especially in recent tourist hotspots like Cancún, is nothing to ignore. One would expect to find a similar underlying hostility among locals toward tourists at popular Mexican beach destinations the likes of which Jamaica Kincaid describes regarding tourism in Antigua. In *A Small Place*, Kincaid writes that "when the natives see you, the tourist, they envy you, they envy your ability to leave your own banality and boredom, they envy your ability to turn their own banality and boredom into a source of pleasure for yourself."[9] But more than overt resentment for the "ugly American" tourist is its more commonplace effect: the adoption of foreign cultural practices. Not necessarily harmful, the interchange between host and guest usually results in the co-optation of "the foreign" into national culture. These can range from democratic values to capitalist practices that include the consumption of new foods and drinks like hotdogs, soda pop, and cocktails, music, and clothing styles. The reverse can also happen; that is, crafts and souvenirs brought back by tourists might spark new trends like the embroidered Latin American folk dress that became popular in the United States in the 1930s and 1940s or the increasingly popular salsa clubs one now finds across central Europe. Whether obvious or subtle, tourism transforms people, communities, and nations. For this reason, tourism remained central to the development programs of both the Mexican and U.S. governments during and after the period covered here.

*   *   *

As this study has shown the government's decision to make tourism an official national industry in late 1928 mirrored broader efforts to diversify and modernize the national economy as well as improve Mexico's relationship with its closest and most contentious neighbor, the United States. Mexico's tourist developers, many of whom comprised the revolutionary elite, learned from a series of studies carried out by 1929 that this "invisible export" proved a panacea to underdevelopment and isolationism experienced during its years of revolutionary fighting. A clear departure from agricultural production and other primary exports, the development of tourism relied on an advanced network of roads, railways, ports and, later, airports as well as first-class accommodations to house and entertain visitors in search of a holiday. Tourism meant modernization and was developed as such by government officials and private entrepreneurs who believed it to be Mexico's ideal route toward domestically led economic development. Although it seemed to contradict revolutionary goals, its developers successfully defined it and even bolstered its cause within the parameters of the revolution. Although the construction of tourist infrastructure remained, at least until the mid-1940s, largely in Mexican hands and under Mexico's control, tourist developers looked to Americans for know-how and support. What emerged was a wide network of cooperation between individuals, businesses, and government agencies in Mexico and the United States who rallied around or profited from tourist development. Together, they marketed an image of Mexico to American tourists as a combination of quaint, productive, and cosmopolitan symbols, which succeeded in attracting an impressive number of tourists by the close of World War II. The gradual ability to attract foreign, especially American, tourists meant that Mexico finally enjoyed international esteem and a reputation as a stable and democratic nation, despite expressions of revolutionary nationalism.

This study of the development of Mexico's tourist industry offers an entry point into understanding the role that economic development played during the years of revolutionary reconstruction and state building. In the name of the revolution, leaders sought to develop an industry that catered not only to the foreign but also benefited national interests, including its economy, politics, society, and culture. Tourist developers and promoters between the years 1928 and 1945 struck what they believed to be a balance that did not sacrifice the revolution to foreign economic, political, and cultural interests. Little did they know that the flaws inherent in tourism would compromise these goals.

APPENDIX A

Table A.1 Tourist entry (mostly American) into Mexico

Years	Tourists
1929	13,892
1930	23,769
1931	41,271
1932	36,964
1933	39,541
1934	63,739
1935	75,432
1936	92,092
1937	130,091
1938	102,866
1939	127,822
1940	125,569
1941	165,627
1942	90,398
1943	126,905
1944	120,218
1945	156,550
1946	254,844
1947	239,756
1948	254,069
1949	306,065
1950	384,297

Note: Statistics can be found in Departamento de Turismo, *Estadísticas básicas* (Mexico: 1973), 1, located at the current library and archive of the Mexican Tourism Department in Polanco, Mexico City. Documents housed there begin in the 1960s. We can assume that the majority of these figures reflect the entry of American tourists, especially before the 1960s. Even by the early 1970s, economist G. Donald Jud estimates that 89% of all tourists in Mexico were from the United States. See G. Donald Jud, "Tourism and Economic Growth in Mexico since 1950," Inter-American Economic Affairs, 28:1 (Summer 1974).

Source: Dirección General de Estadística, *Anuarios estadísticos, 1930–1971*.

NOTES

INTRODUCTION

1. Invitation found in the Archivo Histórico "Genaro Estrada" de la Secretaría de Relaciones Exteriores (hereafter SRE), III-244-4.
   Speech reprinted in *Mexican Art & Life*, 4 (October 2, 1938).
2. Ibid.
3. I refer to these political elites, who were part of what Frank Brandenburg describes as members of the "revolutionary family," as the revolutionary elite borrowing from Thomas O'Brien's apt description in *The Revolutionary Mission: American Enterprise in Latin America, 1900–1945* (Cambridge: Cambridge University Press, 1996). See Frank Brandenburg, *The Making of Modern Mexico* (Englewood Cliffs, NJ: Prentice-Hall, 1964).
4. O'Brien, The *Revolutionary Mission*, 311.
5. Dennison Nash, "Tourism as a Form of Imperialism," in *Hosts and Guests: The Anthropology of Tourism*, ed. Valene Smith (Philadelphia: University of Pennsylvania Press, 1989), 37–52.
6. Nora Hamilton, *The Limits of State Autonomy: Post-Revolutionary Mexico* (Princeton: Princeton University Press, 1982), 84.
7. "Mexico: Travel & Tourism Forging Ahead," The 2004 Travel & Tourism Economic Research, World Travel & Tourism Council (2004).
8. Ibid.
9. I use revolutionary to describe the state, its projects, and those involved, borrowing on the way in which they described themselves at the time. I am aware that much of what was revolutionary was hardly that as Ilene V. O'Malley has pointed out in her work. She argues that because the government lacked a particular ideology under which the revolution fell, they used this term "revolutionary" as a "historical adjective" rather than to describe a kind of revolutionary agenda. See Ilene V. O'Malley, *The Myth of the Revolution: Hero Cults and the Institutionalization of the Mexican State, 1920–1940* (New York: Greenwood Press, 1986), 116–117.
10. See O'Malley, *The Myth of the Revolution*.
11. Luis Cabrera, "The Mexican Revolution—Its Causes, Purposes and Results," a speech given at the American Academy of Political and Social Science and the Pennsylvania Arbitration and Peace Society on

November 10, 1916. The published version can be found in "The Purposes and Ideals of the Mexican Revolution," *The Annals of the American Academy of Political and Social Science*, 69 (January 1917), 1–21.

12. See Mary K. Vaughn, *Cultural Politics in Revolution: Teachers, Peasants, an Schools in Mexico, 1930–1940* (Tucson: University of Arizona Press, 1997) and Rick A. López, "The India Bonita Contest of 1921 and the Ethnicization of Mexican National Culture," *Hispanic American Historical Review*, 82:2 (May 2002), 291–328.

13. Juan B. Rojo, "The Meaning of the Mexican Revolution," in "The Purposes and Ideals of the Mexican Revolution," 27–29.

14. Hamilton, *The Limits of State Autonomy*, 209–213.

15. Men like Emilio Portes Gil, Aarón Sáenz Garza, Luis Cabrera, Luis Montes de Oca, Alberto J. Pani, Rafael Buelna, Pascual Ortíz Rubio, and Lázaro Cárdenas to name only a few.

16. Tourist is defined as one who travels for pleasure. In 1931, the agreed upon definition of a tourist was as follows: "The citizen or national of any contracting state who without intention of establishing his private commercial or industrial residence, nor in the fulfillment of an official function, nor with purely scientific purposes, enters temporarily in the territory of any of the contracting states with the sole object of knowing the country, enjoying its climate or obtaining an objective impression of its customs, scenery, or other attractions of any kind." Harry W. Frantz, "Tourism will be Developed in S. America," *El Universal* (October 29, 1931), 9.

17. On the tenth anniversary of Alemán's death, Héctor Manuel Romero wrote the pamphlet entitled, "Miguel Alemán Valdés (1905–1983): Arquitecto del turismo en México" (México, D.F.: Sociedad Mexicana de Geografía y Estadística, 1993).

18. Miguel Guajardo Bonavides, *Relatos y desarrollo del turismo en México* (México: Miguel Angel Porrua, 1995) whose cover has a portrait of an aged Miguel Alemán; José Rogelio Álvarez, "El turismo," in *México: 50 años de revolución*, I (México: Fondo de Cultura Económica, 1963), 61–64.

19. Other recent studies on tourism include Alex Saragoza, "The Selling of Mexico, Tourism and the State," in *Fragments of a Golden Age: The Politics of Culture in Mexico Since 1940*, ed. Gilbert M. Joseph et al. (Durham: Duke University Press, 2001), 91–115 and Eric Zolov, "Discovering a Land 'Mysterious and Obvious': The Renarrativizing of Postrevolutionary Mexico," in *Fragments of a Golden Age: The Politics of Culture in Mexico since 1940*, ed. Gilbert M. Joseph et al. (Durham: Duke University Press, 2001), 234–272. For insightful narratives on tourism that accompanied art exhibits, see Andrea Boardman, *Destination México: "A Foreign Land a Step Away," U.S. Tourism to México, 1880s–1950s* (Dallas: DeGolyer Library, Southern Methodist University, 2001) and James Oles, *South of the Border: Mexico in the*

American Imagination, 1914–1947 (Washington, DC: Smithsonian Institution Press, 1993).

20. In particular, anthropologist Valene Smith's cohort and sociologists like John Urry and Dean MacCannell.

21. Valene Smith, "Introduction," in *Hosts and Guests: The Anthropology of Tourism*, ed. Valene Smith (Philadelphia: University of Philadelphia Press), 1.

22. Hal K. Rothman, *Devil's Bargain: Tourism in the Twentieth-Century American West* (Lawrence: University of Kansas Press, 1998), 30.

23. Rothman, *Devil's Bargain*, 31.

24. John Urry, *The Tourist Gaze: Leisure and Travel in Contemporary Societies* (London: Sage Publications, 1990), 2–3.

25. An example of this in 2003 saw France's tourist industry plummet when Jacques Chirac refused to join the United States in its war in Iraq and, as a result, many U.S. tourists refused to travel there.

1   MEXICO'S NEW REVOLUTION: THE RACE FOR THE TOURIST DOLLAR, 1928–1929

1. Jean A. Meyer argues that 1929 marked the transition from revolutionaries to state officials. See Jean Meyer, *The Cristero Rebellion: The Mexican People Between Church and State, 1926–1929* (London: Cambridge University Press, 1976).

2. Anonymous, "Mexico Makes Bid for Tourist Trade," *New York Times* (July 8, 1929).

3. Anonymous, "Mexico Wants Visitors," *Philadelphia Public Ledger* (July 9, 1929). Since the Porfirian era (1876–1910), military men accompanied passenger and cargo trains. Since banditry was rampant in border areas, the protection of railways was necessary for cargo to arrive unharmed. During the violent era of the revolution (1910–1917), insurgents often derailed trains in search of money and ammunition to fund their armies. Those U.S. visitors and businessmen, who traveled by coach at the turn of the century, fell victim to bandits so much so that most tourists throughout the period under investigation in this study (1928–1946) believed Mexico to be dangerous. As a result, tourism promoters in Mexico worked hard to change impressions of their nation from "barbaric" to "modern." See chapters 2 and 4.

4. Frank Brandenburg first used the concept of the "Revolutionary Family" in *The Making of Modern Mexico*. Like other scholars of Mexico from the 1960s, his agenda was to prove that the revolution in Mexico still existed. And, Mexico was exemplary because its revolution initiated democracy and progress. Despite his agenda, "Revolutionary Family" is useful because it suggests the consolidation of Mexico's new elite held together by friendship, self-interest, and dedication to the idea of the revolution. Tourist pioneers who organized, developed, and promoted this industry between 1928 and 1946

reflected broader membership in the family and were able to forge ties across the republic and in the United States. Again, they did so within the limits of revolutionary goals. For a discussion of the "Revolutionary Family," see Frank Brandenburg, *The Making of Modern Mexico* (Engelwood Cliffs, NJ: Prentice Hall, 1994).

5. In a letter sent to President Portes Gil, Felipe G. Cantón, a Mexican living in New York, wrote that Mexico should take advantage of the new relationship forged by Morrow and Lindbergh to develop commercial and intellectual ties between the Untied States and Mexico. See Archivo General de la Nación, Grupo Documental: Emilio Portes Gil (hereafter AGN: EPG), 41:2/302/104 (January 1, 1929).

6. The most important highway was the Nuevo Laredo-Mexico City Highway that linked the Untied States to central Mexico by 1936 (later called the Pan-American Highway). This highway's many names— Nuevo Laredo-Mexico City Highway, Laredo-Mexico City Highway, and Pan-American Highway—changed depending on who wrote the document, whether from a North American or Mexican. In 1937, the Nuevo Laredo-Mexico City Highway underwent an official name change to the Pan-American Highway when the Pan-American Union began plans to construct the section from Mexico City to Guatemala.

7. See the presidential decree that created the CMPT, published in the *Diario Oficial* on July 11, 1929.

8. Refers to the *Ley de Protección del Tesoro Artístico e Histórico de México* passed in 1936 by President Cárdenas. This law stated that all objects from 1521 to 1821 were considered national treasures and gave the state the right to expropriate any would-be protected object in poor condition. Academics and officials from related ministries determined its artistic and historic value.

9. The regulations passed in the 1930s in these cities explain why today visitors to Taxco and Pátzcuaro find only colonial-style buildings with orange roofs and white walls.

10. Statistics on metal exports, oil production, and its value published by the Ministry of Finance. Centro de Estudios de Historia de México CONDUMEX, Fondo: Luis Montes de Oca (hereafter CEHM: LMDO), 199/18574 (December 16, 1930).

11. Personal notes from Luis Montes de Oca. CEHM: LMDO, 200/18682 (December 1930).

12. Cuba figure from Rosalie S. Schwartz, *Pleasure Island: Tourism and Temptation in Cuba* (Lincoln: University of Nebraska, 1997), 88.

13. Transcript of radio program, "El vocero de Mexico," aired on XEN Radio Station. CEHM: LMDO, 199/18580 (December 17, 1930). For a look at how this perception related to developing and regulating sex tourism, see Katherine Elaine Bliss, *Compromised Positions: Prostitution, Public Health, and Gender Politics in Revolutionary Mexico City* (University Park, PA: Penn State University Press, 2001), 163–164.

14. Letter from the Chamber of Commerce in Laredo, Texas to Andrés Landa y Piña of Interior Ministry reprinted in the "Boletín para la sesion del dia 17 de septiembre de 1929." Archivo Histórico "Genaro Estrada" de la Secretaría de Relaciones Exteriores (hereafter SRE), IV-299-11: I; Anonymous, "La industria del turismo en México," *Excélsior* (July 26, 1929).

15. Dudley was commissioned by railway companies to study the state of hotels in Mexico. "Tentative Report of Mr. Frank A. Dudley, President of the United States Hotel Company of America, Respecting the Establishment of a Chain of First Class Hotels in Mexico." AGN: Pascual Ortíz Rubio (hereafter AGN: POR), 35, 1, 144/104: 14793 (November 28, 1930).

16. E. Ferreira, consul in San Diego, "Informe correspondiente a diciembre de 1924" (Num. 43), published in *Boletín comercial*, a publication of the SRE (March 20, 1925), 9–10.

17. José Damaso Fernández, consul general in Havana, "El turismo en Cuba," Report of May 1926 (Num. 177), in *Boletín commercial*, a publication of the SRE (June 26, 1926), 4–5.

18. All reports made between the years 1928 and 1929 can be found in SRE, IV-300-1: IV (for consulates in the United States and the Americas) and V (for consulates in Europe). The criterion for the reports is taken from the following: Ismael Vázquez, consul general in Galveston, Texas, "Informe por junio de 1928." SRE, IV-300-1: IV (July 10, 1928).

19. A.V. Martínez of the Mexican Consulate in Phoenix, AZ, "Informe especial sobre el turismo." SRE, IV-300-1: IV (August 24, 1928).

20. A. Casarín of the Mexican Consulate in St. Louis, MO, "Turismo." SRE, IV-300-1: IV (July 19, 1928).

21. L. Lupián of the Mexican Consulate in Chicago, IL, "Turismo." SRE, IV-300-1: IV (August 8, 1928).

22. L. Peña of the Mexican Consulate in Del Rio, TX, "Informe por junio de 1928." SRE, IV-300-1: IV (July 20, 1928).

23. Edmundo González Roa of the Mexican Consulate in Prague, Czechoslovakia, "Turismo: Informe especial." SRE, IV-300-1: V (July 24, 1928).

24. Report made to the CPT on April 30, 1929 by Ing. José Rivera of the National Road Commission, A.L. Rodríguez of the Banco de Mexico, S.A. and vice-president of the CPT, and José Manuel Ramos of the Industry and Commerce Ministry, compiled in a brochure entitled, "Acta Constitutiva, Estatutos y Dictámes of the Asociacion Automovilística Mexico-Americana of Monterrey." AGN: EPG, 41, 2/302/104:17532.

25. José Damaso Fernández of the Mexican Consulate in Toronto, Canada, "Informe correspondiente al mes de marzo de 1929: La industria del turismo y los intereses fiscales." SRE, IV-168-54 (April 13, 1929). Natural Resources Intelligence Service Department

of the Interior, "How to Enter Canada: Summary of the regulations regarding the entry of automobiles for touring, pleasure boats, tourists' outfits and travellers' baggage." No date but presumably 1929 based on other contents in series. SRE, IV-168-23; and, letter from Charles Mumm, secretary of the Laredo Chamber of Commerce and later director of the American Automobile Association in Texas to the Ministry of Foreign Affairs. SRE, IV-299–11: I (October 1, 1929).

26. Statistics from the Banco de México, Departamento de Turismo, "Estadística de los automoviles de turistas que han entrado a México por la aduana de Nuevo Laredo para dirigirse a Monterrey o recorrer la carretera, durante los meses mayo, junio, julio, y agosto del presente año." SRE, IV-300-1: II (September 5, 1929).

27. Juan Sánchez Azcona, "La industria del turismo en Cuba," *La revista nacional de turismo*, 1: 1 (June 1930), 30, 64–65. SRE, IV-300-1: VI.

28. Report regarding tourism sent to Ministry of Foreign Affairs by Manuel Álvarez of the Mexican Consulate in Havana, Cuba. SRE, IV-300-1: IV (August 11, 1928).

29. At first, when the Interior Ministry brought together officials who would recommend a protocol for the entry of tourists at Mexico's borders in late December 1928, the private sector had been ignored. It is believed that only days after the CPT was founded, Andrés Landa y Piña, head of the Interior Ministry's Statistics Department, changed its name to CMPT to make room for participation from private enterprise. Among the few studies of Mexico's tourist industry, none mention the CPT and all begin their narrative with the CMPT in 1929. This is no doubt an error because it overlooks the government's sense of uncertainty about tourism development as well as the valiant efforts by private individuals before 1929. For clarity (and stubbornness), the author refers to the CPT as the unofficial organization before July 1929, and the CMPT as the official organization after July 1929.

30. The rotating presidents included Emilio Portes Gil, Pascual Ortíz Rubio, and Abelardo L. Rodríguez. During the *Maximato*, a term used to signify the ruling power behind the presidents, revolutionary general and former president Plutarco Elías Calles. Each president took office only to resign (generally by force) within two years.

31. Letter from A. Mascareñas to the Ministry of Foreign Affairs introducing the bank's Department of Tourism and naming Antonio L. Rodríguez as the head of it. SRE, IV-300-1 IV.

32. Brochure produced in 1929 but without a specific date. Sent to Ministry of Foreign Affairs with an attached note from Mascareñas. SRE, IV-168-54.

33. It states, "Many of the former pupils of the Summer School are acquainted with Mexico City, but it is not generally known that Mexico City is the ideal place where to spend your vacations." Brochure produced in 1929 but without a specific date. Sent to Ministry of Foreign Affairs. SRE, IV-300-1: II (February 20, 1929).

34. Produced in 1932 but without a specific date. SRE, IV-492–29.
35. Memorandum to CMPT from Mascareñas dated September 4, 1929. SRE, IV-300–1: II.
36. Ibid.
37. The author has only found one sample of a Bank of Mexico tourism stamp during her research at SRE, III-495–23. To be sure, these stamps were a hit among consul generals, for several demanded that the bank send more. See SRE, IV-492–29.
38. Mascareñas resigned his position as director on May 25, 1932 in a letter addressed to Plutarco Elías Calles, who was president and founder of the bank when it was established in 1925 at Alberto J. Pani's suggestion. Pani, the Treasury Minister, argued to centralize the nation's money and banking system. The gossip behind Mascareñas' resignation is that he had too much personal interest in the bank, that is, he defaulted on loans. This and other information about the bank was kindly shared with the author in several meetings with Eduardo Turrent Díaz, the bank's historian, who helped the author understand banking in Mexico and the Bank of Mexico's involvement in tourism. Also see Eduardo Turrent Díaz, *Historia del Banco de México*, Vol. I (México: Banco de México, 1982) and Vol. II (México: Banco de México 2001).
39. Incidentally, the bank and the federal government were already intimately linked, as the latter owned a little more than half its shares, while bankers, including Mascareñas himself, industrialists, and other banking institutions owned the rest. Despite this close relationship, the bank and its directors exercised autonomy as a corporation, or Sociedad Anónima (S.A.), until 1982 when the peso crisis forced the government to nationalize it.
40. Predecessor to Mexico's most prominent tourism organization, Asociación Mexicana de Turismo (AMT) founded in 1939.
41. List compiled from reports by Mexican Consulate in New York sent to SRE on October 22 and November 22, 1928 announcing the creation of the MTA. SRE IV-299–11: I.
42. Letter from José Miguel Bejarano to C.L. Hunter. SRE, IV-300–1: II (November 15, 1928).
43. The commission was organized on December 14, 1928. Anonymous, "Historia de la Comisión Nacional de Turismo," *La revista nacional de turismo*, 11–15.
44. Report by Head of the Statistics Department for the Interior Ministry and Secretary of the CPT, Andrés Landa y Piña, "El turismo en México: Lo que se refiere para fomentarlo." SRE, IV-299–11: II. (December 14, 1928).
45. The laws dealing with border entry all fall under articles in the *Ley de Migración* decreed on January 15, 1926 and September 8, 1927.
46. The Mexican press quickly publicized the founding of this organization. See "Para el desarrollo del turismo en México y EU," *El Universal* (January 10, 1929).

47. From report presented to the CPT by Rodríguez, Rivera and Ramos. AGN: EPG, 41, 2/302/104: 17532 (April 20, 1929).
48. From AAMA, "Acta constitutiva, estatutos y díctames." AGN: EPG, 41, 2/302/104:17532 (August 8, 1929).
49. Report to CPT by Customs Section, which included José Manuel Ramos, José Rivera R. and Bernardo Iturriaga. SRE, IV-300–1: V (April 22, 1929).
50. "Circular for Health Agents at Ports and Borders," written by Dr. A. Ayala, Head of the Department of Public Health and representative to CPT. AGN: EPG, 41, 2/302/104:17532.
51. Memorandum to CPT from Antonio L. Rodríguez on February 21, 1929. SRE, IV-300–1: II.
52. *México: Guia de turismo* I: 1 (July 1929). SRE, IV-300–1: VI.
53. Comment made by Ministry of Health representative to CPT, Enrique Monterrubio, at their meeting on June 11. From "Acta de la decima octava sesión ordinaria celebrada el dia 11 de junio de 1929." Secretaría de Gobernación, México, D.F. SRE, IV-299–11: I.
54. Portes Gil signed the law but it was actually decreed on January 30, 1930 and published in the *Diario Oficial* on February 7, 1930. Despite the entrance of President Ortíz Rubio, Portes Gil remained president of the CNT at least until the end of 1930. During the Great Depression, 1930–1934, the CNT was not active and no records of meetings after the summer 1930 are found. The same goes for additional groups of the CNT, namely the Patronato and Comité Oficial, that were created in 1933 under President Abelardo L. Rodríguez.
55. Most of these early tourism groups emerged from local groups in the states of Michoacán, Colima, Coahuila, Aguascalientes, Yucatán, San Luis Potosí, Baja California, Guadalajara, Tabasco, and Querétero. Information compiled by the author from various sources including: SRE, IV-300–1: II; Anonymous, "Comisiones en las principales ciudades," *El Universal* (March 1, 1929); Anonymous, "En Aguascalientes se impulsara," *El Universal* (March 2, 1929); and Anonymous, "Existe una junta impulsora en Mérida," *El Universal* (June 2, 1929).

2 STATE SUPPORT AND PRIVATE INITIATIVE: PATTERNS IN THE DEVELOPMENT AND PROMOTION OF TOURISM, 1930–1935

1. Borja Bolado, former editor for *El Economista*, worked closely with Luis Montes de Oca at this publishing house. Montes de Oca probably owned shares in Editorial Mercurio.
2. *MAPA* became the official automobile and motor tourism magazine of the AMA in 1933.

3. The number of questionnaires sent out and responses returned is unknown. Centro de Estudios de Historia de México CONDUMEX, Fondo: Luis Montes de Oca (hereafter CEHM: LMDO), 169/16265.

4. According to many sources from 1928 to 1930, this was the expected inauguration date until the Great Depression caused its delay.

5. This was discussed by Finance Minister Luis Montes de Oca as early as 1928. It never panned out due to financial constraints on the ministry. Ironically, Montes de Oca established the Crédito Hotelero in 1937, a private lending firm comprised of money from banks.

6. Letter from Julio Novoa to Luis Montes de Oca, regarding his recent conversation with Puebla governor, General Almazán, in which the governor was angry that the Secretary of Communications and Public Works (SCOP) cancelled contracts for roads. CEHM: LMDO, 256/23637 (March 9, 1932); letter from Bernardino Ramirez to Luis Montes de Oca regarding the situation in Taxco where the majority of the highway to the city was complete and awaiting gasoline services but where certain sections, especially from Taxco to Cacahuamilpa, could not be finished. CEHM: LMDO, 260/24066 (May 23, 1932); and Ing. Joaquin Pedrero Cordova to Luis Montes de Oca, August 23, 1932, regarding his work on the highway from Mérida to Chichen-Itzá, which was almost nearly complete but could not be finished due to lack of funding. CEHM: LMDO, 263/24346.

7. W.M. Wattles of the *New York Times* to Ortíz Rubio proposing a publicity campaign and subsequent response by the president. Archivo General de la Nación, Grupo Documental: Pascual Ortíz Rubio (hereafter AGN: POR), 78 (January 13, 1931), 144/2133. Enrique D. Ruiz to Rodríguez, July 7, 1933, and subsequent response from his personal secretary July 20, 1933. AGN: Abelardo L. Rodríguez (hereafter AGN: ALR), 99, 505.2.25: 17158 and 15655.

8. See table A.1, appendix A.

9. In Helen Delpar, *The Enormous Vogue of Things Mexican: Cultural Relations between the United States and Mexico, 1920–1935* (Tuscaloosa: University of Alabama, 1992), 58, Delpar argues that inexpensive travel to Mexico is what sustained the industry during depression years. While this may in part be true, it does not explain why there is a noticeable increase in the rate of foreign tourists entering Mexico between 1930 (23,769) and 1931 (41,000). This chapter sheds light on those individuals whose efforts directly reshaped negative perceptions of Mexico.

10. Anonymous, "Lo que pide el turismo," *Excélsior* (June 4, 1929).

11. "La industria del turismo en México," *Excélsior* (July 26, 1929); *El economista* (June 17, 1929).

12. Mexican Consular Edgardo L. Burchell, in Providence, RI, to Secretaría de Relaciones Exteriores (SRE) in 1928, L. Peña, and A.V. Martínez. SRE, IV-300–1/ IV.

13. Mexican Consular Edmundo González Roa in Prague to SRE in 1928. SRE, IV-300–1/V.
14. Lewis McBride to Luis Montes de Oca. CEHM: LMDO, 197/18454 (November 26, 1930); Lewis McBride, "Memorandum in regard to the detention of Mr. T. Douglas Robinson at Nogales, Mexico." CEHM: LMDO, 197/18455 (November 26, 1930).
15. Philip Welhausen, "Made Trip into Mexico," *Daily Herald* (July 20, 1932), Yoakum, TX.
16. They referred to environmental conservation as "the conservation of typical customs of race like fauna and flora." Enrique Couttolenc, "Proyecto de reglamento del Primer Congreso Nacional de Turismo." SRE, IV-97–14 (April 1930).
17. Eduardo de León, "Proyecto presentado al Primer Congreso Nacional de Turismo," on April 23, 1930. SRE, IV-97–14.
18. Alberto B. Girard, "Trabajo presentado en el Primer Congreso Nacional de Turismo de México." CEHM: LMDO, 180/17016 (April 23, 1930).
19. "Discurso del Señor Secretario de Hacienda Luis Montes de Oca pronunciado en la sesión del Congreso Nacional de Turismo el dia 25 de abril de 1930." CEHM: LMDO, 180/17029, 17030 (April 25, 1930).
20. Still today, the government works to combat fears among tourists in Right of warnings posted by the U.S. State Department regarding the increasing violence in Mexico and danger of taxi-cab crime, highway or "express" kidnappings, and robberies at ATM machines. To allay fears among American tourists, Mexico has established official tourist offices across the United States, has employed U.S. publicity agents to produce propaganda, and has used personal contacts with travel writers at American newspapers. These warnings are from the U.S. State Department's website, www.state.gov, which would scare prospective tourists to Mexico.
21. "American Woman Killed in Mexico: Tourists Attacked," *The Times* (August 30, 1924) in Fideicomiso Archivos Plutarco Elías Calles y Fernando Torreblanca: Plutarco Elías Calles, 1103, 87: I.
22. Samuel Ramos, *El perfil del hombre y la cultura en México* (México: Imprenta Mundial, 1934).
23. Transcript of XEN radio program, "El vocero en México," Ing. Felix Palavicini. CEHM: LMDO, 185/17490 (June 27, 1930).
24. Transcript of XEN radio program, "El vocero en México," Ing. Felix Palavicini. CEHM: LMDO, 199/18580 (December 17, 1930).
25. Speech given by Luis Montes de Oca to National Bankers' Convention. CEHM: LMDO, 215/20038 (April 22, 1931).
26. Letter from director of XEN, Fernando Leal Novelo, to Luis Montes de Oca introducing new program entitled, "Hora impulsora de las actividades nacionales." CEHM: LMDO, 228/21301 (August 11,

1931); letter from R. Lopes del Rosal, organizer of exposition, to Montes de Oca. CEHM: LMDO, 212/19712 (March 24, 1931).

27. Alberto B. Girard, "Trabajo presentado en el Primer Congreso Nacional de Turismo de México." CEHM: LMDO, 180/17016 (April 23, 1930).

28. The National Tourism Commission, *La revista nacional de turismo*, I: I (June 1, 1930).

29. V.C. Mc. Dunn, "Our Welcome," *La revista*, 37.

30. Colonel C.D. Hicks, "Tourist Business," *La revista*, 41 and 58.

31. R.J. Eustace, "The Fine Auto Roads of Mexico," *La revista*, 44–45.

32. Ibid., 45.

33. President Pascual Ortíz Rubio, "Para el primer numero de La revista nacional de turismo," *La revista*, 6–7.

34. Riva Palacio does not explicitly state how tourism would transform the minds of Mexicans. However, it is not farfetched to assume that he most likely refers to its modernizing effect. What might that mean? Well, although the definition of modernity is ever changing, in the early 1930s it meant economic and political stability so as to develop into an industrialized nation.

35. Statements by CNT members compiled in an essay entitled, "El criterio de Gobernación sobre el turismo," *La revista*, 10.

36. Anonymous, "Nuestros propósitos," *La revista*, 19.

37. Ing. Felix Palavicini, "Puntos de vista sobre el turismo," *La revista*, 24 and 80.

38. While the Bank of Mexico's Department of Tourism disappeared after Mascareñas left, when former Treasury Minister Luis Montes de Oca was invited in 1934 (after his resignation in 1932) as director of the bank, he did not reopen the department but worked fervently on behalf of the bank to promote and develop tourism. See chapter 3.

39. Asociación Mexicana Automovilística, "Informe General: Correspondiente al ejercicio social de 1933." IV Asamblea General Ordinaria, Monterrey, N.L. CEHM: LMDO, 274/25416 (December 20, 1933).

40. By the late 1930s in a propaganda ploy, the Mexican government sponsored Chavez's is tour in the Untied States where he performed with symphony orchestras in Chicago, Boston, and New York City.

41. See Delpar, *The Enormous Vogue of Things Mexican*, 60: 73–76.

42. The exhibition took place on April 18–25 at the Grand Central Palace in Manhattan. CEHM: LMDO, 211/19669 (March 21, 1931).

43. CEHM: LMDO, 270/25050 (July 20, 1933) and 271/25111 (August 19, 1933).

44. Carlos A. de la Vega, "Turismo," *El Nacional* (January 20, 1938).

45. Letter from Colonel Hicks, president of the Missouri Pacific Railroad Company in Mexico, to sub-secretary of the Interior, Felipe Canales. SRE, IV-300-1: II (no exact date but in 1929).

46. Letter from Alexandria, LA mayor, V.V. Lamkin, to President Portes Gil. AGN: EPG, 41, 2/302/104, 15140 (November 8, 1929).
47. Letter from L.W. Baldwin of Missouri Pacific Railroad Company of the United States to Robert J. Eustace in which he thanks Eustace for organizing the lecture series and offers support for the cause. CEHM: LMDO, 101/10233 (May 29, 1928).
48. Transcribed speech by Dr. Lincoln Wirt sent to President Portes Gil in hopes of publication in Spanish by the official Press Department. AGN: EPG, 9, 315/104, 14004 (September 6, 1929).
49. Comments by Luis Duplan, consul general and Ministry of Foreign Affairs' delegate to the CMPT. From news service, Agencia Mexicana Trens. SRE, IV-299–11: I (December 4, 1929).
50. William L. Vail, "Seeing Mexico," *Los Angeles Times* (September 12, 1930).
51. Articles sent by Leslie W. Tuttle to President Cárdenas. Published in the editorial section of the *Tacoma News Tribune* (December 6–7 and 13–15, 1934).
52. SRE, IV-495-4 (1932). Likewise, the publicity department at the Mexican Power and Light Company published two maps of Mexico City and surrounding areas that, too, was sent to consulates in the United States for distribution. See SRE, IV-499-29 (April 14, 1932).
53. AGN: POR, 78 (1931), 144, 2190 (March 14, 1931).
54. Letter from M.F. Hoyle to President Ortíz Rubio, AGN: POR, 35 (1930), 1, 144/104, 2575 (March 1, 1930).
55. AGN: POR, 78 (1931), 144, 2133 (January 13, 1931). Incidentally, the Mexican state could not afford this kind of proposal until 1939 when Cárdenas poured money into a U.S. campaign to promote tourism through the press. Mexico's official and private sector was simply not financially secure enough by the early 1930s to hire a U.S. publicity agent.
56. Letter from Joseph Eller to General Calles on December 11, 1932. Fideicomiso Archivos Plutarco Elías Calles, Archivo Plutarco Elías Calles, 1748, 19, 3/6; CEHM: LMDO, 227/21063 (July 21, 1931).
57. Proposal from F. Martínez Madrazo to Ignacio García Tellez. SRE, IV-300-1: V (no specific date).
58. Proposal from José J. Razo to President Ortíz Rubio. AGN: POR, 35 (1930), 1, 144/104, 9577 (July 20, 1930); Proposal from Bolaños to President Ortíz Rubio. AGN: POR, 78 (1931), 144, 3426 (April 27, 1931).
59. Enrique D. Ruiz to President Ortíz Rubio. AGN: POR, 35 (1930), 1, 144/104, 12539 (October 10, 1930).
60. Javier Gaxiola to Enrique D. Ruiz. AGN: ALR, 99, 505.2/25, 15655 (July 20, 1933).
61. Dr. O. Friedlieb, "San Antonio de los Buenos de Mendoza." CEHM: LMDO, 170/16278 (January 1930).

62. Letter of introduction from Orozco to Ortíz Rubio. CEHM: LMDO, 179/16916 (April 2, 1930).

63. For a biography of Gore and his family who moved to Mexico City from the United States in the late nineteenth century, see William Schell Jr., *Integrated Outsiders: The American Colony in Mexico City, 1876–1911* (Wilmington: SR Books, 2001), 53.

64. Tómas Gore asked the government to exempt him from taxes on materials imported from the United States for the renovations made to Hotel Geneve in 1931. Minister of Finance, Luis Montes de Oca, and the head of the Departamento del Distrito Federal (DDF), Lamberto Hernandez, approved his request. See CEHM: LMDO, 212/19777 and 19800 (March 20, 1931).

65. Frank A. Dudley, "Tentative Report of Mr. Frank A. Dudley, President of the United States Hotels Company of America, Respecting the Establishment of a Chain of First Class Hotels in Mexico," (November 28, 1930). AGN: POR, 35 (1930), 1, 144/104, 14793.

66. Annex to proposal submitted by President Rodríguez and Pani. CEHM: LMDO, 281/26052 (September 6, 1932).

67. "Propuesto global para la construcción del 'HOTEL PALACE' en la Ciudad de México," (September 18, 1935).

68. Figures compiled by Roberto López of the National Railways of Mexico, "Datos sobre el negocio de hoteles en México." CEHM: LMDO, 281/26055 (October 1, 1935).

69. Ing. Alberto J. Pani, *Obsesiones y recuerdos* (México, D.F.: n.p., 1953). Gift to author from personal library of Enrique Pani. Also see Frank R. Brandenburg's brief but informative section on the hotel industry in *The Making of Modern Mexico* (Englewood Cliffs, NJ: Prentice Hall, 1964).

3 MOTORING TO MEXICO: HIGHWAYS, HOTELS, AND *LO MEXICANO*, 1936–1938

1. This highway is also referred to in the documents as the Nuevo Laredo-Mexico Highway, the San Antonio-Mexico City Highway, and the Laredo-Mexico Highway. Today, this highway is one small part of the Pan-American Highway that extends through Central America.

2. Itinerary drafted by head of the Communications and Public Works Ministry (hereafter SCOP), Francisco J. Múgica, Centro de Estudios de Historia de Mexico CONDUMEX, Fondo: Luis Montes de Oca (hereafter CEHM: LMDO), 288/16692 (January 15, 1936).

3. Figures from Asociación Mexicana Automovilística (hereafter AMA), Consejo Nacional. CEHM: LMDO, 347/32293 (October 14, 1938).

4. Statistics from automobile historian John B. Rae, *The Road and the Car in American Life* (Cambridge, MA: MIT Press, 1971), 50. Also

see Rae's earlier work, *The American Automobile: A Brief History* (Chicago: University of Chicago Press, 1965), 238.

5. For a pertinent discussion about tourism, motor travel, and the making of American identity, see Marguerite S. Shaffer, *See America First: Tourism and National Identity, 1880–1940* (Washington: Smithsonian Institution Press, 2001).

6. For a good historigraphical discussion on Cárdenas, see Adrian A. Bantjes, *As if Jesus Walked on Earth: Cardenismo, Sonora, and the Mexican Revolution* (Wilmington: SR Books, 1998), xi–xv; and Alan Knight, "Cardenismo: Juggernaut or Jalopy?" *Journal of Latin American Studies*, 26:1 (February 1994), 73–107.

7. Historians are beginning to shed light on Cárdenas as a capitalist. See Thomas O'Brien, *The Revolutionary Mission: American Enterprise in Latin America, 1900–1945* (Cambridge: Cambridge University Press, 1996) and Julio Moreno, *Yankee Don't Go Home! Mexican Nationalism, American Business Culture, and the Shaping of Modern Mexico, 1920–1950* (Chapel Hill: University of North Carolina Press, 2003).

8. Enrique Krauze, *Mexico, Biography of Power: A History of Modern Mexico, 1810–1996* (New York: Harper Perennial, 1997), 416.

9. For a more in-depth discussion of this new class, see Nora Hamilton, *The Limits of State Autonomy: Post Revolutionary Mexico* (Princeton: Princeton University Press, 1982). Hamilton argues that a new capitalist class emerged out of the revolutionary elite. Many of these so-called capitalists were also tourist developers and promoters.

10. A traditional *china poblana*, a regional type from Puebla, wears a skirt with sequins and the Mexican eagle in the center, an embroidered blouse embossed with colorful thread and glass beads, a silk or cotton *rebozo* (shawl), and red shoes. A traditional *charro*, horseman and rodeo performer, wears a tailored suit trimmed with embroidery and silver buttons, a soft tie, and sombrero.

11. Report on the conference, January 19–24, 1936, in Cleveland, Ohio from the head of the Department of Tourism, Ignacio L. Hijar. CEHM: LMDO, 285/26373 (March 7, 1936).

12. Copy of speech given to Pan-American session. CEHM: LMDO, 285/26373 (January 21, 1936).

13. Ignacio L. Hijar, "Estudio presentado por el C. Ignacio L. Hijar, Jefe del Departamento del Turismo de la Secretaría de Gobernación, sobre las condiciones que presenta el turismo norteamericano en general con relación a Mexico." CEHM: LMDO, 285/26372 (March 7, 1936).

14. The AMA was not the first motor club to form in Mexico. Before 1929, the National Automobile Association (ANA) already existed in Mexico City. As far as the author can tell from the documents, the ANA did not play a role in fomenting international tourism to Mexico before 1946 but helped foment national tourism, a topic discussed in chapter 5. Few documents on tourism mention the ANA, even the

rich sources from the AMA. The author has found part of an *Anuario turístico* (tourist yearbook) in Spanish and English for 1947.

15. Asociación Mexicana Automovilística, "Informe General: Correspondiente al ejercicio social de 1933." IV Asamblea General Ordinaria, Monterrey, Nuevo León. CEHM: LMDO, 274/25416 (December 20, 1933).

16. Minutes from the Asamblea General Ordinaria de la AMA, Club del Distrito Federal. CEHM: LMDO, 343/31934 (August 1, 1938).

17. Prominent Mexican journalist and nightlife reporter, Carlos Denegri, cited in Stephen Niblo's book, *Mexico in the 1940s: Modernity, Politics, and Corruption* (Wilmington, DE: SR Books, 1999), 66–67. Niblo uses Denegri's comment to argue that the revolution shifted entirely by the 1940s. This study on the promotion and development of Mexico's tourist industry is informed by the idea that the revolution did not shift by the 1940s because progress and modernization was always a key revolutionary goal, something that has been overshadowed by the agrarian aspect of the revolution. See Nora Hamilton, *The Limits of State Autonomy* for a convincing argument about revolutionary capitalists.

18. Montes de Oca remained unmarried and often traveled with his nieces.

19. Letter of invitation from Luis Montes de Oca to Davey Tree Experts in June 1938. CEHM: LMDO, 339/31634.

20. CEHM: LMDO, 295/27333 (November 26, 1936).

21. Most of these books he ordered from the Fondo de Cultura Económica. Some of the titles he bought included: A.J. Norval, *The Tourist Industry* (London: Sir Isaac Pitman & Sons, Ltd., 1936); F.W. Ogilvie, *The Tourist Movement: An Economic Study* (London: P. S. King & Sons, Ltd., 1933); Marcel Gautier, *L'Hotellerie: Etude Theorique et Pratique*; Angelo Mariotti, *Corso di Economia Turistica* (Novara: Instituto geografico de Agostini, 1933); and, D.J. O'Brien, *Hotel Administration: Accounts and Control.* CEHM: LMDO, 350/32605 (December 10, 1938).

22. Festival itinerary. CEHM: LMDO, 301/27725 (January 1, 1937).

23. List compiled from meeting minutes. CEHM: LMDO, 289/26799 and 289/26815 (July, 1936).

24. Minutes from a meeting of the AMA Club of Mexico City. CEHM: LMDO, 343/31934 (August 1, 1938).

25. CEHM: LMDO, 289/26828 (July 29, 1936).

26. CEHM: LMDO, 290/26860 (August 2, 1936).

27. Managers from both oil companies were also members of the AMA and sat on its AMA's Tourism Committee.

28. CEHM: LMDO, 291/26960 (September 4, 1936).

29. Based on a series of telegrams sent to delegations beginning on September 11, 1936. CEHM: LMDO, 291/26983–26989.

30. Members of the AMA local and national councils accused AAA president, Charles Mumm, of spreading misnomers about the danger of travel in Mexico after the 1938 oil nationalization.
31. "Informe del Sr. Luis Montes de Oca, Presidente del Consejo Nacional de la Asociación Mexicana Automovilística." CEHM: LMDO, 318, 29420 (July 26, 1937).
32. Copy of article by Santa Marina G., "Renglones sueltos," found in archive but can be located as well in *MAPA*, 31. See CEHM: LMDO, 293/27176 (October 1936).
33. Luis Montes de Oca, "Servicio, no servidumbre," *Boletín nacional de información*, 16. CEHM: LMDO, 323/29930 (October 1937).
34. From another letter to hoteliers entitled, "El tiempo del turista," *Boletín nacional de información*, 19 and 20. CEHM: LMDO, 333/31040 (February and March 1938).
35. Anonymous, "El turismo va a recibir un serio impulso," *El Nacional* (August 26, 1938), 8.
36. CEHM: LMDO, 320/26973 (August 24, 1937).
37. CEHM: LMDO, 328/30470 (December 15, 1937).
38. The AMH still exists today under the name, the Mexican Hotel and Motel Association and the National Chamber of Hotels (AMHM-CNH). They are located on Balderas. The author would like to thank Juan Manuel Olivares Rivera for allowing her to consult their collection of *Hoteles mexicanos* and for providing her with useful contacts in Mexico City.
39. The author would like to thank Jaime Barceló, head of the EMT, for providing the author with pamphlets on the history of this school as well as discussing the current state of Mexico's tourist industry.
40. Patrice Olsen, "Saving the Past, Denying the Present? Cárdenas, Development, and Preservation in Mexico City, 1934–1940" (paper presented at the annual meeting of the Rocky Mountain Council for Latin American Studies, Santa Fe, New Mexico, January 2000) and Patrice Olsen, "Artifacts of the Revolution: Architecture, Society and Politics in Mexico City, 1920–1940," (Ph.D. diss., Penn State University, 1998).
41. Quevedo initially called the group the Valley of Mexico Grand Tourism Committee because, he wrote, Mexico City was the nation's primary tourist zone. CEHM: LMDO, 291/26981 (September 9, 1936). Only two months later, the name was changed to the more inclusive National Tourism Committee.
42. CEHM: LMDO, 293/27115 (September 17, 1936).
43. CEHM: LMDO, 292/27012 (September 18, 1936).
44. The word he used to describe "native" art is "autóctono," which could be taken to mean indigenous art of Mexica and Mayan past or, more generally, art that comes from Mexico.
45. The revolutionary creed is discussed by Frank R. Brandenburg, *The Making of Modern Mexico* (Englewood Cliffs NJ: Prentice Hall,

1964), 7–18. This study of tourism does not subscribe completely to Brandenburg's framework but shows the "Revolutionary Family" and "creed" at work. More than anything, the creed points to prevailing revolutionary goals that shaped the era of reconstruction and institutionalization of the revolution after 1929 and as early as 1925.

46. CEHM: LMDO, 293/27115 (September 17, 1936).
47. Ibid.
48. CEHM: LMDO, 330/30786 (January 30, 1938).
49. J.F. Orozco Escobosa, "Memorandum para el Comité Nacional de Turismo." CEHM: LMDO, 332/30989 (February 23, 1937).
50. Del Valle joined the ranks of Montes de Oca, Tómas Gore, Frank Sanborn, and Emilio Azcárraga who were members of this commission. CEHM: 323/29937 (October 1, 1937) and 323/29989 (October 9, 1937).
51. CEHM: LMDO, 330/30786 (January 30, 1938).
52. "Proyecto del programa de actividades del Comité Nacional de Turismo durante el año de 1937." CEHM: LMDO, 315/29167 (June 30, 1937).
53. Copy of the *Ley de Protección del Tesoro Artístico e Histórico de México* decreed by President Lázaro Cárdenas. CEHM: LMDO, 299/27584 (December 31, 1936).
54. Ing. Felix M. Escalante, "Algunas consideraciones sobre la convivencia de conservar el caracter típico de las poblaciones," paper presented at the Planning Congress held in Mexico City. CEHM: LMDO, 171/16280 (January 1930).
55. Enrique Couttolenc, "El establecimiento de ciudades balnearios," paper presented at the Planning Congress held in Mexico City. CEHM: LMDO, 172/16414 (January 1930).
56. Ángel Roldan, "Arboledas urbanas," papers presented at the Planning Congress. CEHM: LMDO, 172/16386. Ing. M.A. de Quevedo, "Los espacios libres en las ciudades y su adaptación a parques, jardineas y lugares de juego." CEHM: LMDO, 172/16386 (January 19, 1930).
57. In both these neighborhoods, those parks built during the 1920s and 1930s are still filled with jacarandas.
58. Ing. Leopoldo Vazquez, "Proposiciones presentadas al Congreso Nacional de Planeación para mejorar al aspecto de la Ciudad de México." CEHM: LMDO, 172/16389 (January 20, 1930).
59. A synthesized copy of his reports can be found in CEHM: LMDO, 294/27253 (November 10, 1936). Older ones can be found in CEHM: LMDO, 259/23923; 261/24123; and 261/24155.
60. Letter from Luis Montes de Oca to Jacques H. Lambert. CEHM: LMDO, 260/24073 (May 24, 1932).
61. Letter to Montes de Oca from Efraín Buenrostro of the Finance Ministry who requested, some weeks earlier, copies of Lambert's studies. CEHM: LMDO, 295/27318 (November 21, 1936).
62. CEHM: LMDO, 296/27390 and 296/27421 (December 16, 1936).

63. Arq. Vicente Mendiola Q. Speech given at the 6th Convention of the AMA (2nd for the AMA-Mexico City Club). CEHM: LMDO, 288/26676 (June 8–9, 1936).

64. Felipe Sánchez used this term in 1938 to describe the destruction of gardens and parks in Mexico City. See CEHM: LMDO, 335/31260 (April 11, 1938). Francisco Borja Bolado also used this term in 1937 in reference to Taxco. See CEHM: LMDO, 301/27797 (January 27, 1937).

65. Arq. Vicente Mendiola Q., Ing. Armando Santacruz, Jr., Ing. José Gama, and Arq. Luis Prieto Souza, "Comisión de Planeación de Nuevo Laredo, Tamps.: Programa de obras. 1937 a 1937." CEHM: LMDO, 317/29317 (July 15, 1937).

66. Ibid.

67. Thelma and Blinn Yates, "To Mexico by Motor," *New York Times* (April 3, 1937).

68. Letter from Furlong to George H. Copeland, travel editor of *New York Times*. CEHM: LMDO, 307/28341 (April 26, 1937).

69. Ibid.

70. The author's documents give no clear indication about the readership of "The Furlong Service." They suggest that this newsletter was sent to motor clubs throughout the United States. Because Furlong reported to Montes de Oca, president of the AMA National Council, he included as often as possible praiseworthy testimony of his activities, especially his newsletter and presentations. For example, see CEHM: LMDO, 326/30278 (November 22, 1937).

71. William H. Furlong, "The Furlong Service." CEHM: LMDO, 289/26797 and 323/29993 (July 18, 1936 and October 12, 1937).

72. Report from Furlong to Montes de Oca. CEHM: LMDO, 308/28419 (May 3, 1937).

73. CEHM: LMDO, 320/29605 (August 16, 1937).

74. CEHM: LMDO, 320/29671 (August 24, 1937).

75. William H. Furlong, "Partial Report." CEHM: LMDO, 295/27339 (November 26, 1936). Each month or two, Furlong sent a report to Luis Montes de Oca in order to keep him and the AMA abreast of his activities.

76. William H. Furlong, "The Furlong Service." CEHM: LMDO, 317/29313 (July 15, 1937).

77. William H. Furlong, "Partial list of publications which have accepted and published two to ten photographs furnished by this organization." CEHM: LMDO, 323/29931 (October 1, 1937).

78. William H. Beezley and Colin M. MacLachlan, *El gran pueblo: A History of Greater Mexico*, 2nd ed. (Upper Saddle River, NJ: Prentice Hall, 1999), 351.

79. Figures from Juan S. Farías, secretary of AMA-Monterrey Club, "Memorandum sobre la disminuición del turismo y sus efectos en la economia nacional." CEHM: LMDO, 343/31971 (August 6, 1938).

80. See Lorenzo Meyer, *Mexico and the United States in the Oil Controversy, 1917–1942* (Austin: University of Texas, 1972), 213–214 and Moreno, *Yankee Don't Go Home!*, 53.

81. Bulletin sent to Luis Osio y Torres Rivas from Albert Nathan of Houston, TX. Archivo Histórico "Genaro Estrada" de la Secretaría de Relaciones Exteriores (hereafter SRE), III-244–4 (August 17, 1938).

82. Letter from Mary B. Bookmeyer to William H. Furlong forwarded to Luis Montes de Oca. CEHM: LMDO, 337/31454 (May 12, 1938).

83. Transcript of radio broadcast sent to Luis Montes de Oca. Program was aired on radio stations in Memphis, Little Rock, Fort Smith, El Dorado, Hot Springs, Siloam Springs, and St. Louis. CEHM: LMDO, 337/31439 (May 10, 1938).

84. Report from Mejia to President Cárdenas. Archivo General de la Nación, Grupo Documental: Lázaro Cárdenas (hereafter AGN: LC), 548.2/1 (May 29, 1938).

85. Letter from William H. Furlong to the Ministry of Foreign Affairs dated August 24, 1938. He included a clipping from the San Antonio News entitled, "Tourist Data Inimical to San Antonio and Mexico Corrected." SRE, III-244-4 (August 22, 1938).

86. Eduardo Hay, Minister of Foreign Affairs, wrote Ambassador Daniels seeking compensatory action against oil companies. Bluntly, Daniels wrote that U.S. civil liberties allowed for the freedom of speech and press and that oil companies were in some ways justified considering that the Mexican government had not yet compensated owners of expropriated properties. SRE, III-244-4 (October 3, 1939).

87. AMA, "Boletin a la prensa, hoteles, turistas y público en general," CEHM: LMDO, 345/32121 (September 1, 1938).

88. José Rivera R. CEHM: LMDO, 345/32185 (September 19, 1938). Report made to the AMA National Council regarding recent weather problems and stranded tourists.

89. Incidentally, American writer Elizabeth Forsythe Hailey writes about this incident in *Woman of Independent Means* (New York: Penguin Books, 1998), a novel told through a series of letters that was first published in 1978. The main character, Bess, was stranded in Cuidad Monte, Mexico while driving from Texas to Mexico along the Pan-American Highway in late August 1938. In letters to her daughter who has just given birth to her first grandchild, Bess writes that she is not sure she will make it out of Mexico alive with the tragic flooding along the highway that made all bridges impassable. She writes that because hotels were overflowing with stranded tourists, she and others were sent to one of the largest sugar mills in Tampico where its owners set up cots. She writes that tourists were without means of communication for days on end and that food was indeed scarce. She was finally able to reach Monterrey when the governor of Tampico commandeered a tractor to take the most desperate tourists to

Victoria where they could catch a bus to Monterrey and a train to Texas.

90. CEHM: LMDO, 345/32131 (September 4, 1938). This folder includes telegrams and a signed letter from 30 tourists who returned safely to the United States.
91. Anonymous, "Suffering Reported among Americans Stranded in Mexico," *San Antonio Express* (September 4, 1938).
92. Copy of KMOX radio broadcast. CEHM: LMDO, 345/32130 (September 3, 1938).

4 "VACATIONING WITH A PURPOSE": TOURISM PROMOTION ON THE EVE OF WORLD WAR II

1. "Mexico—The Faraway Land Nearby" is the title of a tourism brochure written in English in 1939 by Howard Phillips expressly for reproduction by the Mexican Tourist Association (hereafter AMT) who printed 100,000 copies of this 48-page pamphlet. For figures on AMT publication numbers see Centro de Estudios de Historia de México CONDUMEX, Fondo: Luis Montes de Oca (hereafter CEHM: LMDO), 373/34383 (December 17, 1939). For a text-only version of "Mexico—The Faraway Land Nearby," see CEHM: LMDO, 363/33550 (June 10, 1939). The author found an original copy purchased at a used bookstore on Donceles in Mexico City.
2. Dorothy Reinke to President Ávila Camacho, on August 12, 1941. Archivo General de la Nación, Grupo Documental: Manuel Ávila Camacho (hereafter AGN: MAC), 548.3/4.
3. See Seth Fein, "Everyday Forms of Transnational Collaboration: U.S. Film Propaganda in Cold War Mexico," in *Close Encounters of Empire: Writing the Cultural History of U.S.-Latin American Relations*, ed. Gilbert M. Joseph et al. (Durham: Duke University Press, 1998), 400–450.
4. See table A.1, appendix A.
5. See John Mason Hart, *Empire and Revolution: The Americans in Mexico since the Civil War* (Berkeley: University of California Press, 2002), Chapter 13 but especially 414–417; Stephen R. Niblo, *War, Diplomacy, and Development: The United States and Mexico, 1938–1954* (Wilmington: SR Books, 1995); and Julio Moreno, *Yankee Don't Go Home! Mexican Nationalism, American Business Culture, and the Shaping of Modern Mexico, 1920–1950* (Chapel Hill: University of North Carolina Press, 2003). Moreno's study in particular illustrates the ways in which American corporations doing business in Mexico, like Sears, had to accommodate to Mexicans.
6. AMT manager, Lucas de Palacio wrote a three-page press release entitled, "Vacationing with a purpose." AGN: MAC, 704/170–1 (September 28, 1942).

7. Ibid.

8. Don Short to the *New York Journal-American*, December 12, 1941, and printed in Spanish in the *Boletín de la Asociación Mexicana de Turismo* (hereafter *B-AMT*), IV:1 AGN: MAC, 704/170-1 (January 8, 1942).

9. Alfonso Teja Zabre the head of the new *Dirección General de Información* explained the agency's duties in a letter of introduction to Luis Montes de Oca. CEHM: LMDO 378/34664 (January 11, 1940). Also see William H. Beezley and Colin M. MacLachlan, *El gran pueblo: A History of Greater Mexico* (Upper Saddle River, NJ: Prentice-Hall, 1999), 347–348 and Michael Miller, *Red, White, and Green: The Maturing of Mexicanidad, 1940–1946* (El Paso: Texas Western Press, 1998), 67 and 71.

10. Department of Press and Publicity (DAPP), "The Valley of Mexico" (DAPP: México, 1937), located in the library of the Centro de Estudios de la Historia de México CONDUMEX.

11. The centrality of Mexico City on which Mexico's entire tourist industry rested is explored in chapter 5.

12. Lic. José Rivera P.C., *Publicidad turística de México* (DAPP: México, 1939) located in the Biblioteca de México: Fondo México. Lic. José Rivera should not be confused with Ing. José Rivera R. who was intimately involved in tourism since the late 1920s as an important member of the National Highway Commission, AMA, AMT, and National Chambers of Commerce.

13. *The Miami Herald* (December 25, 1937), 9-B. Also found in AGN: President Lázaro Cárdenas (hereafter AGN: LC), 548.2/1.

14. Ibid.

15. For more on Furlong, see chapter 3.

16. Antonio Pérez O., "Informe rendido por el Sr. Antonio Pérez de la Caravana de buena voluntad de Los Greeters Mexicanos." CEHM: LMDO, 319/29518 and 343/31946 (June 4–July 6, 1938).

17. Lucas de Palacio, "La Asociación Mexicana de Turismo, su origen, su plan de acción," paper presented at the Rotary Club's Technical Congress on Tourism held in March 1939. CEHM: LMDO, 356/33088; Scott Hardy, vice-president of the Texas Hotel Association, "Report: Mexico-Texas Relations," submitted to Luis Montes de Oca. CEHM: LMDO, 358/33216 (April 5, 1939).

18. Members of these hotel associations included many of the same hoteliers and managers with whom Pérez's Hotel Greeters met in Atlantic City only months earlier.

19. Invitation from President Cárdenas, Archivo Histórico "Genaro Estrada" de la Secretaría de Relaciones Exteriores (hereafter SRE), III-244-4 (October 2, 1938).

20. Minutes of first AMT meeting. CEHM: LMDO, 355/32960 (February 7, 1939).

21. "Magnifica labor de propaganda turista," *Excélsior* (April 29, 1937), 10.

22. J.F. Orozco Escobosa, "Memorandum para el Comité Nacional de Turismo." CEHM: LMDO, 332/30989 (February 23, 1937).
23. CEHM: LMDO, 334/31134 (March 19, 1938).
24. Francisco C. Lona, "Labores inmediatas y concretas de la AMT." CEHM: LMDO, 355/33008 (February 20, 1939).
25. AMT report on contributions. CEHM: LMDO, 365/33710 (July 15, 1939). For an example of an issue with contributors, see CEHM: LMDO, 385/35331 (May 14, 1940).
26. Lucas de Palacio, "Special Bulletin concerning the Fundraising Campaign." CEHM: LMDO, 384/35227 (April 20, 1940).
27. CEHM: LMDO, 384/35227 (April 20, 1940) and CEHM: LMDO, 385/35331 (May 14, 1940).
28. Memorandum from the AMT Publicity Commission. CEHM: LMDO, 363/33549 (June 9, 1939).
29. David S. Oakes, "Sunshine over the Border," reprinted in *Migración, población, turismo*, 1:3 (October 25, 1940), 49–58.
30. CEHM: LMDO, 363/33549 (June 9, 1939).
31. Posters reprinted in *Migración, población, turismo*, 4:28 (October 12, 1943) with Hollywood stars standing by their side. Originals of these posters are currently for sale at Poster Plus in Chicago, IL and fetch a high price. I'd like to thank Poster Plus Gallery for showing me their collection of original Mexican tourist posters.
32. I came across a few AMT Spanish-language brochures on Veracruz, Querétaro, Guadalajara, and Guanajuato in DeGolyer Library at Southern Methodist University. See the Ephemera Collection: A2597, A2598, A2600, and A2616.
33. Memorandum compiled by Scott Hardy, José Rivera R., F. Alatorre, Belisario Quiroz, and F.C. Lona during a meeting at the Hotel Baker, Mineral Wells, Texas. CEHM: LMDO, 373/34383 (December 17, 1939).
34. Press release by Betty Kirk for the Hamilton Wright Organization, Inc. CEHM: LMDO, 388/35535 (June 14, 1940). Cost of AMT spending on publicity campaigns included in the Administrative Council's report. See CEHM: LMDO, 387/35518 (June 13, 1940). Lucas de Palacio announced this campaign in a press release to travel agents. See CEHM: LMDO, 388/35527 (June 14, 1940).
35. The Caples Company was an advertising firm owned by John Caples, one of the most famous advertising and marketing figures in U.S. history.
36. AMT yearly report and prospectus for 1940. CEHM: LMDO, 381/34977 (January 24, 1940), 8.
37. Ibid. Also see CEHM: LMDO, 357/33151 (March 28, 1939).
38. Transcript of radio broadcast. CEHM: LMDO, 365/33654 (July 7, 1939).
39. CEHM: LMDO, 370/33984 (September 4, 1939).

40. Report to the General Council of the AMT. AGN: MAC, 704/170-1 (July 7, 1941). Transcripts of these radio programs are housed at the Center for American History at the University of Texas, Austin.

41. As Julio Moreno has argued, advertising was perceived by government officials during this period as the key to economic growth, especially within an industry like tourism. Moreno, *Yankee Don't Go Home!*, 25.

42. Its administration included Mexicana Airlines owner Aarón Sáenz Garza (president), Salvador J. Romero of FFCCN (vice-president), hotelier Luis Osio y Torres Riva (secretary), Professor Jesús Silva Herzog of Pemex (spokesperson), and Banker Roberto Casas Alatriste (Observation Committee). Roberto Casas Alatriste represented several banking institutions including the Banco de México, Banco de Londres y México, and the Banco General de Capitalización. Casas Alatriste stood in for Luis Montes de Oca who surprisingly established the AMT but did not sit on its Board of Directors and was not formally part of the AMT's day-to-day operations. List of its Administrative Council contained in report by Lucas de Palacio, AMT manager. CEHM: LMDO, 371: 34217 (October 31, 1939).

43. CEHM: LMDO, 370/34003 (September 11, 1939) and 370/34043 (September 21, 1939).

44. CEHM: LMDO, 371/39217(October 31, 1939).

45. *Boletín de la Asociación Mexicana de Turismo*, 20. CEHM: LMDO, 371/34124 (October 9, 1939).

46. "President Cárdenas Proclamation Declaring 1940-41 Travel Years." CEHM: LMDO, 378/34756 (January 29, 1940).

47. Ibid.

48. The first IATC meeting took place in San Francisco, California.

49. For a list of invited countries and for all papers regarding the organization of this congress see SRE, III-428-4: I.

50. "Yes! *We Are Ready!*" (emphasis in original) in *Migración, Población, Turismo*, 1:6 (February 1, 1940), 39-45.

51. Ibid.

52. "President Cárdenas' Straightforward Statements on Mexico's Attitude Toward Travel, as given to Press Correspondents on May 22, 1940." CEHM: LMDO, 378/34756; Spanish version reprinted in the *Boletín de la Asociación Mexicana de Turismo*, 2:9 (May 22, 1940) in SRE, III-428-4: I. Original telegram from President Cárdenas to E.H. Dignowity of the *Daily New Deal* (an English-language newspaper in Mexico City) with attached press release located at the AGN: LC, 548/14 (May 22, 1940). Printed version in the *Daily New Deal*, 1:86 (August 9, 1940) with headline on front page: "CARDENAS PUTS TOURIST TRAVEL FIRST FOR BETTER INTERNATIONAL RELATIONS."

53. Report made by Francisco C. Lona and J.J. March, "Entrevista con el Sr. Presidente de la República Gral de Division Lázaro Cárdenas." CEHM: LMDO, 387/35492 (June 7, 1940). For proof that the donation really made its way into the AMT's treasury, see a letter of confirmation from the Finance Ministry to the president on July 5, 1940. AGN: LC, 548/14.
54. Lucas de Palacio, "A los agentes de turismo en México." CEHM: LMDO, 388/35527 (June 14, 1990).
55. Press release by Betty Kirk. CEHM: LMDO, 388/35535 (June 14, 1940).
56. Report to AMT management. AGN: MAC, 704/170–1 (June 15, 1941).
57. Dr. Osgood Hardy, chair of the History Department at Occidental College in Los Angeles, CA. "El nuevo panamericanismo," speech given to the Los Angeles Publicity Club at the Biltmore Hotel. CEHM: LMDO, 376/34550 (July 2, 1940).
58. Anonymous, " 'Presidential Tour' Comes to Mexico," *Pemex Travel Club*, III:118-A (March–April 1941).
59. Mexican delegates included the following: Alejandro Buelna, Jr., William H. Furlong, Lucas de Palacio, José Rivera R., Francisco C. Lona, J.J. March, Ing. Carlos Bazán (SCOP), Gral. Octavio de la Peña (owner of Washington Apartments in Mexico City), Antonio Pérez O., and Antonio Malo (Hotel Colonial and future owner of Tony's Bar in Mexico City). The author has yet to find a list of U.S. delegates apart from important members of the AAA and the delegate spokesperson, Clarence Werthan, secretary and manager of the Rocky Mountain Motorists, Inc., located in Denver, CO. For a description of the entire itinerary see the report compiled by Pancho Scanlan and Jerry Ryan, "Presidential Tour to Mexico," *A.A.A. Travel News* from the National Touring Bureau. American Automobile Association. AGN: MAC, 704/701–1 (April 24, 1941).
60. The two officials included Lic. Fernando Casas Alemán (Mexico City's next governor during Alemán's presidency) and Lic. Alejandro Gómez Maganda.
61. Antonio Ruiz Galindo had been a member of the revolutionary family since the early 1920s. Always a businessman, he turned hotelier in 1941 and eventually became president of the Mexican Hotel Association. In 1946, he was named National Economic Minister at which time he and Lucas de Palacio founded the Escuela Mexicana de Turismo (EMT), or Mexican Tourism School. Today, his son Antonio Jr. remains honorary president of the EMT in Mexico City.
62. This and other day-to-day activities planned for the delegates on the Presidential Tour can be found in Pancho Scanlan and Jerry Ryan, "Presidential Tour to Mexico," *A.A.A. Travel News* from the National Touring Bureau. American Automobile Association. AGN: MAC, 704/701–1 (April 24, 1941).

63. Ibid.
64. AMT press release dated April 16, 1941. AGN: MAC, 704/170-1.
65. Ibid.
66. Report to the AMT Administrative Council. AGN: MAC, 704/ 170-3 (October 28, 1942).

5 Pyramids by Day, Martinis by Night: Selling a Holiday in Mexico

Parts of this chapter appear in a forthcoming book chapter entitled, "A Drink Between Friends: Mexican and American Pleasure Seekers in 1940s Mexico City," in *Adventures into Mexico: American Tourism Beyond the Border*, ed. Nicholas Bloom (Rowman & Littlefield, in press, 2006).

1. Tana de Gamez and Arthur R. Pastore, *Mexico and Cuba on Your Own* (New York: R.D. Cortina Co., 1954), 7.
2. *The New Yorker* (October 16 and 23, 2000), 135.
3. Jane Bussey, "Mexico City in Transition," Travel Section J, *The Miami Herald* (February 18, 2001).
4. By the early twentieth century, tourism in the United States had shifted from elite groups taking Grand Tours to Europe and middle sectors taking romantic tours to Niagara Falls to an entirely new experience of a pleasure vacation to cities like Chicago, Washington, DC, and New York. See Catherine Cocks, *Doing the Town: The Rise of Urban Tourism in the United States, 1850–1915* (Berkeley: University of California Press, 2001) and Edmund Swinglehurst, *Cook's Tours: The Story of Popular Travel* (New York: Blandford Press, 1982).
5. John Jenkins, "Motor Sparks," *Chicago Daily News* (February 9, 1939). Clipping in Centro de Estudios de Historia de México CONDUMEX, Fondo: Luis Montes de Oca (hereafter CEHM: LMDO) 355/32972.
6. Frances Toor, *Frances Toor's Guide to Mexico* (New York: R.M. McBride & Co., 1936) and *Frances Toor's Motorist Guide to Mexico* (Mexico: Frances Toor Studios, 1938).
7. Toor, *Motorist Guide*, 68–69.
8. Frances Toor, *New Guide to Mexico by Plane, Car, Train, Bus and Boat* (Mexico: Frances Toor Studios, 1946).
9. Alex M. Saragoza, "The Selling of Mexico: Tourism and the State, 1929–1952," in *Fragments of a Golden Age: The Politics of Culture in Mexico since 1940*, ed. Gilbert M. Joseph et al. (Durkham: Duke University Press, 2001), 91–115 and Eric Zolov, "Discovering a Land 'Mysterious and Obvious': The Renarrativizing of Postrevolutionary Mexico," in *Fragments of a Golden Age: The Politics of Culture in Mexico since 1940*, ed. Gibert M. Joseph et al. (Durham: Duke University Press, 2001), 234–272.

10. For a broad theoretical discussion on the purpose of cultural inventions see E.J. Hobsbawm and Terence Ranger, eds., *The Invention of Tradition* (Cambridge: Cambridge University Press, 1983). For cases specific to Mexican popular culture see William H. Beezley, Cheryl English Martin, and William E. French, eds., *Rituals of Rule, Rituals of Resistance: Public Celebrations and Popular Culture in Mexico* (Wilmington: SR Books, 1994); for those specific to Latin America see William H. Beezley and Linda A. Curcio-Nagy, eds., *Latin American Popular Culture: An Introduction* (Wilmington: SR Books, 2000).

11. For more detail on this period and subject, see chapter 3.

12. For more detail on this subject, see chapter 4.

13. *Boletín de la Asociación Mexicana de Turismo* (hereafter *B-AMT*) 2:1 (January 15, 1940). CEHM: LMDO, 378/ 34681.

14. This analysis adds to James Oles's treatment of this 1941 tourist poster by Jorge González Camarena in which he argues that the subject's feminine sensuality symbolizes Mexico's domination by the United States, especially through artistic and economic factors. By looking at the way tourist literature from Mexico posited these women with striking symbols of modernity, a more complex analysis emerges. See James Oles, *South of the Border: Mexico in the American Imagination, 1914–1947* (Washington, DC: Smithsonian Institute Press, 1993), 49–51.

15. Howard Phillips, "Mexico—The Faraway Land Nearby." CEHM: LMDO, 37/3/34383 (December 17, 1939), 12.

16. "Yes, We Are Ready!" *Migración, Población, Turismo* 1:6 (February 1, 1940), 39–45.

17. Ibid., p. 45.

18. See chapter 4.

19. Three-page AMT press release written by its manager, Lucas de Palacio, entitled, "Vacationing with a purpose." Archivo General de la Nación, Grupo Documental: Manuel Ávila Camacho (hereafter AGN: MAC) 704/170–1 (September 28, 1942).

20. Report to the Asociación Mexicana de Turismo, Administrative Council. AGN: MAC, 704/170–3 (October 28, 1942). Emphasis in original. Original posters are located at a variety of U.S. holdings including the Library of Congress, Prints and Photographs Division and Harry Ransom Humanities Research Center at the University of Texas at Austin. A digital version of this image is available online at <http://memory.loc.gov/pp/pphome.html>. A clear and colorful version of this poster can also be found in Oles, 51. More recently, the author saw this image reproduced for mass consumption as a refrigerator magnet. The original painting by Jorge González Camarena from which posters were made at Galas de México, S.A. can be found in Museo Soumaya's Galas de México collection. Paintings and posters were exhibited during the 2002 show entitled, "La leyenda de los

cromos. El arte de los calendarios mexicanos del siglo XX en Galas de México." A publication of the exhibit is for sale at the museum. I'd like to thank Mónica López Velarde, museum curator at Soumaya, for showing me original paintings from the Galas collection and for putting me in contact with Jorge González, the son of the well-known Mexican artist. ·

21. For a description of the process and the museum's collection, see the Galas binder in the Museo Soumaya Reference Library.

22. Again, the traditional view that this image of Mexico, portrayed as a buxom woman holding tropical fruit, reflected a "feminized" nation dominated by their neighbor to the north simply does not take into account broader political and economic factors at play on the eve of and during World War II. These factors, the least of which include oil nationalization and a homegrown tourist industry, clearly suggest that Mexico, to a large extent, controlled its own destiny and wisely chose to befriend, but not necessarily to surrender to, an imperial United States. Thus, the image of Mexico personified by a sensual woman on the "*Visit MEXICO*" poster that was produced by a Mexican artist for the government's official tourist department offers more than just another example of imperialistic United States and passive Mexico. Instead, Mexico's tourist promoters and developers, responsible for making this a viable industry in the first place, accentuate, albeit through feminine sexuality, the strength and productivity of their nation. Thank you to Mónica López for her help in analyzing this image.

23. Interview with Jorge González Camarena S., son of painter Jorge González Camarena, Mexico City, July 2003. Incidentally, Jorge told me that the woman who modeled for his father did in fact look like this ideal Mexican woman of striking beauty. In fact, she was his father's sister-in-law and she appears, with some variation, in several different paintings that were made into posters by Galas de México, S.A.

24. See Zolov, "Discovering a Land 'Mysterious and Obvious'."

25. Part of the Library of Congress, Prints and Photographs Division, this poster can be viewed online at http://memory.loc.gov/pp/pphome.html. Also see Oles, 175.

26. SRE, IV-300–1: II (February 20, 1929).

27. Manuel Gamio, "The Transcendental Aspect of Tourism in Mexico," *Mexico: Guia de turismo* I:1 (July 1, 1929).

28. Bank of Mexico tourist pamphlet entitled, "Visit Mexico the Land of Beauty and Romance." SRE, IV-168–54 (1929).

29. The dates included here are from the original brochure that advertised these trips in an effort to emphasize the historical importance of these buildings. Tourist brochure produced by Wagons Lits-Cook Travel Agency in Mexico City, "How to See Mexico and its Surroundings" (1931). SRE, IV-495–4.

30. Report prepared by Roberto López of the National Railways of Mexico. CEHM: LMDO, 281/26055 (October 1, 1935).

31. Figures based on the "Mexico Hotel Directory/Directorio de Hoteles de la República, 1941–1942," produced by the Department of Tourism and Mexican Tourist Association. AGN: MAC, 704/170–3.
32. Report to AMT Administrative Council on October 28, 1942. AGN: MAC, 704/170–3.
33. *B-AMT*, VI:III. AGN: MAC, 704/170–2 (May 1, 1944).
34. *B-AMT*, VIII:IX. AGN: MAC, 704/170–2 (August 1, 1946).
35. Some Pemex travel writers included Elizabeth Borton de Treviño, a journalist who married a Mexican from Monterrey and took Mexican citizenship. See CEHM: LMDO, 355/32984 (February 15, 1939). Other contributing writers included Howard Keys Hollister, Mabel K. Knight, and Doris Heydn. Most of the articles in the earlier editions of this magazine are written by anonymous authors.
36. Distribution figure from report to the Administrative Council of the Mexican Tourist Association. Asociación Mexicana de Turismo AGN: MAC, 704/170–3 (October 28, 1942).
37. Distribution figure from report to the Administrative Council of the Asociación Mexicana de Turismo, Administrative Council. AGN: MAC, 704/170–3 (October 31, 1945).
38. Victoria Marshall, "Mexico Likes America," *Pemex Travel Club*, II:114-A (November 1, 1940).
39. *Pemex Travel Club*, II:113-A (August 1940).
40. Ibid.
41. "Life in Mexico," *Pemex Travel Club*, VI:151-A (August 1, 1944).
42. Sanborn's is a Mexico City landmark that originally opened as a drugstore in 1903 by a California pharmacist, Walter Sanborn, and his brother, Frank Sanborn. It later featured the capital's first soda fountain. In 1918, Sanborn's moved to its famous downtown location in the House of Tiles (*Casa de los azulejos*). Historically, it was and still is a meeting place for U.S. tourists as well as Mexican urbanites for breakfast, lunch, and dinner. In 1946, the Sanborn family sold it to local entrepreneurs, who, in partnership with Walgreen's, have since opened well over 100 Sanborn's restaurants in Mexico. In addition to its restaurants, Sanborn's also sells merchandise from magazines to luggage. For a history of Sanborn's, see Pepe Romero, *My Mexico City and Yours* (New York: Doubleday, 1962), 35–36.
43. In attendance at the inauguration were more than 43,000 people, most from Mexico City and some from abroad. Mexico's president, Manuel Ávila Camacho, attended the ceremony, as did the president of Costa Rica. The racetrack was designed by U.S. architect, John Sloan, at a cost of Mex$10 million, with room for 50,000 including those sitting in the four-tiered grandstand and in the exclusive Jockey Club. "Mexico Conquered by New Sport," *Pemex Travel Club*, V: 141-A (April–May 1943).
44. "Mexico City-Modern Version," *Pemex Travel Club*, II: 112-A (July 1940).

45. "Mexico of a Hundred Disguises," *Pemex Travel Club*, VI: 150-A (June–July 1944).

46. Centro de Estudios de Historia de México CONDUMEX Fondo: Luis Montes de Oca (hereafter CEHM: LMDO), 381/34977 (January 24, 1940).

47. CEHM: LMDO, 373/34283 (December 17, 1939).

48. Report to AMT management. CEHM: LMDO, 378/34741 (January 25, 1940).

49. CEHM: LMDO, 369/33864 (August 5, 1939).

50. Address by Nelson A. Loomis, chief of the Washington Office of the United States Travel Bureau at the annual convention of the "American Hotel Association" Galveston, TX. CEHM: LMDO, 345/32211 (September 26, 1938).

51. Saturino Cedillo to all federal employees. CEHM: LMDO, 293/27172 (October 21, 1936).

52. CEHM: LMDO, 370/34060 (September 25, 1939).

53. "Reglamento del Trabajo para los Empleados de las Instituciones de Crédito y Auxiliares." CEHM: LMDO, 349/32552 (December 29, 1937).

54. J. Mayora, *Boletín de la Asociación Mexicana de Turismo*, III:19, Archivo General de la Nación, Grupo Documental: Manuel Ávila Camacho (hereafter AGN: MAC) 704/170-3 (November 29, 1941).

55. *Boletín de la Asociación Mexicana de Turismo, B-AMT*, IV: 4. AGN: MAC, 704/170-1 (April 30, 1942).

56. AGN: MAC, 740/170-1 (May 1, 1942).

57. Miguel Alemán, "El problema de la industria nacional del turismo," paper presented in Acapulco. AGN, Grupo Documental: Miguel Alemán Valdés, 54.3/239 (October 1945).

58. Taco Bell drew from on film in which a stereotypical Mexican Chihuahua lip-syncs with his owner Cugat.

59. For U.S. depictions of the typical Mexican bandit see John J. Johnson, *Latin America in Caricature* (Austin: University of Texas Press, 1980).

60. Salvador Novo, *Nueva grandeza mexicana* (México: Editorial Hermes, 1946). For English translation see Salvador Novo, *New Mexican Grandeur*, trans. Noel Lindsay (México: Ediciones ERA, 1967).

EPILOGUE

1. Carlos Fuentes, *The Death of Artemio Cruz* (New York: Farrar, Straus & Giroux, 1991), 15. The original publication date of Fuentes's novel was 1962.

2. Ibid., 16–17.

3. Ibid., 16.

4. Ibid., 26.

5. Ibid., 27.

6. Samuel Ramos, *El perfil del hombre y la cultura en México* (México: Imprenta Mundial, 1934) and Octavio Paz, *The Labyrinth of Solitude* (New York: Grove Press, 1985) orig. pub. 1950.

7. See José Emilio Pacheco, *Battles in the Desert & Other Stories* (New York: New Directions Publishing Company, 1987); El Indio's film *Siempre Tuya* (1951); Buñuel's film *Los Olvidados* (1950); and Oscar Lewis's many ethnographies *Five Families: Mexican Case Studies in the Culture of Poverty* (New York: Basic Books, 1959) and *The Children of Sanchez: Autobiography of a Mexican Family* (New York: Random House, 1961).

8. Economist G. Donald Jud, for example, argues that tourism has had little to no negative effect on Mexico. In an article written in 1974, Jud contends that because tourist developers incorporated and preserved local customs, Mexicans experience less resentment toward affluent tourists. See G. Donald Jud, "Tourism and Economic Growth in Mexico since 1950," *Inter-American Economic Affairs*, 28:1 (Summer 1974), 40. Jud narrowly defines negative effect by hostility and anger rather than other factors like cultural change.

9. Jamaica Kincaid, *A Small Place* (New York: Farrar, Straus & Giroux, 1988), 19. Daniel Hiernaux-Nicolas only alludes to this kind of conflict in his essay on Cancún entitled, "Cancún Bliss," *The Tourist City*, ed. Dennis R. Judd and Susan S. Fainstein (New Haven: Yale University Press, 1999), 138–139.

BIBLIOGRAPHY

ARCHIVES AND LIBRARIES

Archivo General de la Nación, Galería Presidencial
  Emilio Portes Gil
  Pascual Ortíz Rubio
  Abelardo L. Rodríguez
  Lázaro Cárdenas
  Manuel Ávila Camacho
  Miguel Alemán Valdés
Archivo Histórico "Genaro Estrada" de la Secretaría de Relaciones Exteriores
Archivo y Biblioteca de la Sociedad Mexicana de Geografía y Estadística
Biblioteca Turística de Héctor Manuel Romero
Biblioteca del Archivo Histórico de la Ciudad de México
Biblioteca Mexicana de la Fundación Miguel Alemán
Biblioteca Miguel Lerdo de Tejada
  Archivos Cortes de Periódico
Biblioteca Museo Soumaya
Biblioteca y Archivo Aarón Sáenz Garza
Centro de Estudios de Historia de México CONDUMEX
  Colección Luis Montes de Oca
DeGolyer Library, Southern Methodist University
  Ephemera Collection
Fideicomiso Archivos Plutarco Elías Calles y Fernando Torreblanca
  Plutarco Elías Calles
Nettie Lee Benson Library, University of Texas at Austin
Universidad Nacional Autónoma de México
  Hemeroteca Nacional

PERIODICALS

Boletín comercial (Ministry of Foreign Affairs)
Boletín de la Asociación de Turismo (Mexican Tourist Association)
La revista nacional de turismo (National Tourism Commission, Interior Ministry)
MAPA (Mexican Automobile Association)
Mexican Art & Life (Department of Press and Publicity)
México: Guía de turismo (Interior Ministry)

Migración, población, turismo (Interior Ministry)
Pemex Travel Club (Petróleos Mexicanos)

NEWSPAPERS

Chicago Daily News
Daily New Deal (Mexico City)
El Nacional
El Universal
Excélsior
Los Angeles Times
Miami Herald
New York Times
Philadelphia Public Ledger
San Antonio Express
Tacoma News Tribune (Tacoma, Washington)

PUBLISHED PRIMARY SOURCES

Asociación Nacional Automovilística. *Anuario turístico.* México: n.p., 1947.

Cabrera, Luis, et al. "The Purposes and Ideals of the Mexican Revolution." *The Annals of the American Academy of Political and Social Science* 69 (January 1917): 1–21.

Departamento Autónomo de Prensa y Publicidad (DAPP). "The Valley of Mexico." Mexico: DAPP, 1937.

De Gamez, Tana and Arthur R. Pastore. *Mexico and Cuba on Your Own.* New York: R.D. Cortina Co., 1954.

Mexican Tourist Association. "Mexico—A Faraway Land Nearby." México: n.p., 1939.

Novo, Salvador. *Nueva grandeza mexicana.* México: Editorial Hermes, 1946.

Pani, Alberto J. *Apuntes autobiográficos exclusivamente para mis hijos.* México, D.F.: n.p., 1945.

———. *Obsesiones y recuerdos.* México, D.F.: n.p., 1953.

Rivera, José. *Publicidad turística de México.* México: DAPP, 1939.

Romero, Héctor Manuel. "Miguel Alemán Valdés (1905–1983): Arquitecto del turismo en México." México: Sociedad Mexicana de Geografía y Estadística, 1993.

———. *Alberto J. Pani, los fabulosos 20's y el turismo en la Ciudad de México.* México, D.F.: n.p., n.d.

Secretaría de Comunicación y Obras Públicas (SCOP), Dirección Nacional de Caminos. *Memoria sobre el camino Mexico-Nuevo Laredo.* México: SCOP, 1936.

Toor, Frances. *Frances Toor's Guide to Mexico.* New York: R.M. McBride & Co., 1936.

———. *Frances Toor's Motorist Guide to Mexico.* Mexico: Frances Toor Studios, 1938.

————. *New Guide to Mexico by Plane, Car, Train, Bus and Boat.* Mexico: Frances Toor Studios, 1946.

SECONDARY SOURCES

Aguilar Camín, Héctor and Lorenzo Meyer. *In the Shadow of the Mexican Revolution: Contemporary Mexican History, 1910–1989.* Austin: University of Texas Press, 1993.

Agustín, José. *Tragicomedia mexicana 1: La vida en México de 1940 a 1970.* México, D.F.: Editorial Planeta de México, 1990.

Álvarez, José Rogelio. "El turismo." In *México: 50 años de revolución* I, 61–64. México: Fondo de Cultura Económica, 1963.

Aron, Cindy S. *Working at Play: A History of Vacations in the United States.* Oxford: Oxford University Press, 1999.

Bantjes, Adrian A. *As if Jesus Walked on Earth: Cardenismo, Sonora, and the Mexican Revolution.* Wilmington: SR Books, 1998.

Beezley, William H., Cheryl English Martin, and William E. French, eds. *Rituals of Rule, Rituals of Resistance: Public Celebrations and Popular Culture in Mexico.* Wilmington: SR Books, 1994.

Beezley, William H. and Colin M. Maclachlan. *El gran pueblo: A History of Greater Mexico.* 2nd ed. Upper Saddle River, NJ: Prentice Hall, 1999.

Beezley, William H. and Linda A. Curcio-Nagy, eds. *Latin American Popular Culture: An Introduction.* Wilmington: SR Books, 2000.

Belasco, Warren James. *Americans on the Road: From Autocamp to Motel, 1910–1945.* Cambridge, MA: MIT Press, 1979.

Bliss, Katherine E. *Compromised Positions: Prostitution, Public Health, and Gender Politics in Revolutionary Mexico City.* University Park, PA: Penn State University Press, 2001.

Boardman, Andrea. *Destination México: "A Foreign Land a Step Away," U.S. Tourism to Mexico, 1880s–1950s.* Dallas: DeGolyer Library, Southern Methodist University, 2001.

Brandenburg, Frank R. *The Making of Modern Mexico.* Englewood Cliffs, NJ: Prentice Hall, 1964.

Cocks, Catherine. *Doing the Town: The Rise of Urban Tourism in the United States, 1850–1915.* Berkeley: University of California Press, 2001.

Couttolenc Urquiaga, Rafael. *Remembranzas de la sociedad capitalina: Ciudad de México, 1930–1960.* México, D.F.: Editorial Diana, 2000.

Delpar, Helen. *The Enormous Vogue of Things Mexican: Cultural Relations between the United States and Mexico, 1920–1935.* Tuscaloosa: University of Alabama, 1992.

Dulles, Foster Rhea. *America Learns to Play: A History of Recreation.* New York: Appleton-Century-Crofts, 1965.

Erenberg, Lewis. *Steppin' Out: New York Nightlife and the Transformation of American Culture, 1890–1930.* Chicago: University of Chicago Press, 1981.

Fainstein, Susan S. and David Gladstone. "Evaluating Urban Tourism." In *The Tourist City,* edited by Dennis R. Judd and Susan S. Fainstein, 21–34. New Haven: Yale University Press, 1999.

Fein, Seth. "Everyday Forms of Transnational Collaboration: U.S. Film Propaganda in Cold War Mexico." In *Close Encounters of Empire: Writing the Cultural History of U.S.-Latin American Relations*, edited by Gilbert M. Joseph et al., 400–450. Durham: Duke University Press, 1998.

Fuentes, Carlos. *The Death of Artemio Cruz*. New York: Farrar, Straus & Giroux, 1991.

Guajardo Bonavides, Miguel. *Relatos y desarrollo del turismo en México*. México, D.F.: Miguel Angel Porrua, 1995.

Hailey, Elizabeth Forsythe. *A Woman of Independent Means*. New York: Penguin Books, 1998 (orig. pub. 1978).

Hamilton, Nora. *The Limits of State Autonomy: Post-Revolutionary Mexico*. Princeton: Princeton University Press, 1982.

Hart, John Mason. *Empire and Revolution: The Americans in Mexico since the Civil War*. Berkeley: University of California Press, 2002.

Hiernaux-Nicolas, Daniel. "Cancún Bliss." In *The Tourist City*, edited by Dennis R. Judd and Susan S. Fainstein, 124–139. New Haven: Yale University Press, 1999.

Hobsbawm, E.J. and Terence Ranger, eds. *The Invention of Tradition*. Cambridge: Cambridge University Press, 1983.

Jud, G. Donald. "Tourism and Economic Growth in Mexico Since 1950." *Inter-American Economic Affairs* 28,1 (Summer 1974): 19–43.

Kandell, Jonathan. *La Capital: The Biography of Mexico City*. New York: Henry Holt and Company, 1990.

Kincaid, Jamaica. *A Small Place*. New York: Farrar, Straus & Giroux, 1988.

Knight, Alan. "Cardenismo: Juggernaut or Jalopy?" *Journal of Latin American Studies* 26,1 (February 1994): 73–107.

———. "The rise and fall of Cardenismo, c. 1930–c. 1946." In *Mexico Since Independence*, edited by Leslie Bethell, 241–320. Cambridge: Cambridge University Press, 1991.

Krauze, Enrique. *Mexico, Biography of Power: A History of Modern Mexico, 1810–1996*. New York: Harper Perennial, 1997.

Lewis, Oscar. *Five Families: Mexican Case Studies in the Culture of Poverty*. New York: Basic Books, 1959.

———. *The Children of Sánchez: Autobiography of a Mexican Family*. New York: Random House, 1961.

López, Rick A. "The India Bonita Contest of 1921 and the Ethnicization of Mexican National Culture," *Hispanic American Historical Review* 82: 2(2002), 291–320.

MacCannell, Dean. *The Tourist: A New Theory of the Leisure Class*. New York: Schocken Books, 1976.

Meyer, Jean. *The Cristero Rebellion: The Mexican People Between Church and State, 1926–1929*. London: Cambridge, 1976.

Miller, Michael Nelson. *Red, White, and Green: The Maturing of Mexicanidad, 1940–1946*. El Paso: Texas Western Press, 1998.

Moreno, Julio. *Yankee Don't Go Home! Mexican Nationalism, American Business Culture, and the Shaping of Modern Mexico, 1920–1950*. Chapel Hill: University of North Carolina Press, 2003.

Mostkoff, Aida. "Foreign Visitors and Images of Mexico: One Hundred Years of International Tourism, 1821–1921." Ph.D. diss., UCLA, 1999.

Nash, Dennison. "Tourism as a Form of Imperialism." In *Hosts and Guests: The Anthropology of Tourism*, edited by Valene Smith, 37–52. Philadelphia: University of Pennsylvania Press, 1989.

Niblo, Stephen R. *War, Diplomacy, and Development: The United States and Mexico, 1938–1954.* Wilmington: SR Books, 1995.

———. *Mexico in the 1940s: Modernity, Politics, and Corruption.* Wilmington: SR Books, 1999.

Nolan, Mary Lee and Sydney. "The Evolution of Tourism in Twentieth-Century Mexico." *Journal of the West* 27 (October 1988): 14–25.

Novo, Salvador. *Nueva grandeza mexicana.* México: Editorial Hermes, 1946.

O'Brien, Thomas. *The Revolutionary Mission: American Enterprise in Latin America, 1900–1945.* Cambridge: Cambridge University Press, 1996.

Oles, James. *South of the Border: Mexico in the American Imagination, 1914–1947.* Washington, DC: Smithsonian Institution Press, 1993.

Olsen, Patrice. "Artifacts of the Revolution: Architecture, Society and Politics in Mexico City, 1920–1940." Ph.D. diss., Penn State University, 1998.

———. "Saving the Past, Denying the Present? Cárdenas, Development, and Preservation in Mexico City, 1934–1940." Paper presented at the annual meeting of the Rocky Mountain Council for Latin American Studies, Santa Fe, New Mexico, January 2000.

O'Malley, Ilene V. *The Myth of the Revolution: Hero Cults and the Institutionalization of the Mexican State, 1920–1940.* New York: Greenwood Press, 1986.

Pacheco, José Emilio. *Battles in the Desert & Other Stories.* New York: New Directions, 1987.

Pattullo, Polly. *Last Resorts: The Cost of Tourism in the Caribbean.* London: Cassell & Co., 1996.

Paz, Octavio. *The Labyrinth of Solitude.* New York: Grove Press, 1985.

Paz Salinas, María Emilia. "México y la defensa hemisférica, 1939–1942." In *Entre la guerra y la estabilidad política: El México de los 40,* edited by Rafael Loyola, 49–64. México, D.F.: Editorial Grijalbo, 1990.

Peralta Sandoval, Sergio H. *Hotel Regis: Historia de una época.* México, D.F.: Editorial Diana, 1996.

Rae, John B. *The Automobile: A Brief History.* Chicago: University of Chicago Press, 1965.

Ramos, Samuel. *El perfil del hombre y la cultura en México.* México: Imprenta Mundial, 1934.

———. *The Road and the Car in American Life.* Cambridge: MIT Press, 1971.

Romero, Pepe. *My Mexico City and Yours.* New York: Doubleday, 1962.

Rothman, Hal K. *Devil's Bargain: Tourism in the Twentieth-Century American West.* Lawrence: University of Kansas Press, 1998.

Saragoza, Alex M. *The Monterrey Elite and the Mexican State, 1880–1940.* Austin: University of Texas Press, 1988.

———. "The Selling of Mexico: Tourism and the State, 1929–1952." In *Fragments of a Golden Age: The Politics of Culture in Mexico Since 1940,* edited by Gilbert M. Joseph et al., 91–115. Durham: Duke University Press, 2001.

Schantz, Eric Michael. "From *Mexicali Rose* to the Tijuana Brass: Vice Tours of the United States-Mexico Border, 1910–1965." Ph.D. diss., UCLA, 2001.

Schell Jr., William. *Integrated Outsiders: The American Colony in Mexico City, 1876–1911.* Wilmington: SR Books, 2001.

Schwartz, Rosalie S. *Pleasure Island: Tourism and Temptation in Cuba.* Lincoln: University of Nebraska, 1997.

Shaffer, Marguerite S. *See America First: Tourism and National Identity, 1880–1940.* Washington: Smithsonian Institution Press, 2001.

Swinglehurst, Edmund. *Cook's Tours: The Story of Popular Travel.* New York: Blandford Press, 1982.

Taylor, Frank Fonda. *To Hell With Paradise: A History of the Jamaican Tourist Industry.* Pittsburgh: University of Pittsburgh Press, 2003.

Torres, Blanca. "La guerra y la posguerra en las relaciones de México y Estados Unidos." In *Entre la guerra y la estabilidad política: El México de los 40,* edited by Rafael Loyola, 65–82. México, D.F.: Editorial Grijalbo, 1990.

Torruco Marqués, Miguel. *Historia institucional del turismo en México, 1926–1988.* México: Asociación Nacional de Egresados de Turismo, 1988.

Turrent Díaz, Eduardo. *Historia del Banco de México,* Vol. I. México: Banco de México, 1932.

———. *Historia del Banco de México,* Vol. II. México: Banco de México, 2001.

Urry, John. *The Tourist Gaze: Leisure and Travel in Contemporary Societies.* London: Sage Publications, 1990.

Vaughan, Mary King. *Cultural Politics in Revolution: Teachers, Peasants, and Schools in Mexico, 1930–1940.* Tucson: University of Arizona Press, 1997.

Vázquez, Josefina Zoraida and Lorenzo Meyer. *México frente a Estados Unidos (Un ensayo histórico 1776–1988).* México, D.F.: Fondo de Cultura Económico, 1989.

Vianna, Hermano. *The Mystery of the Samba: Popular Music and National Identity in Brazil.* Edited and translated by John Charles Chasteen. Chapel Hill: University of North Carolina Press, 1999.

Waters, Wendy. "Re-mapping the Nation: Road Building as State Formation in Post-Revolutionary Mexico, 1925–1940." Ph.D. diss., University of Arizona, 1999.

Weir, L.H. *Europe at Play: A Study of Recreation and Leisure Time Activities.* New York: A.S. Barnes & Company, 1937.

Wilkie, James W. *The Mexican Revolution: Federal Expenditure and Social Change Since 1910.* Berkeley: University of California Press, 1967.

Zolov, Eric. *Refried Elvis: The Rise of the Mexican Counterculture.* Berkeley: University of California Press, 1999.

———. "Discovering a Land 'Mysterious and Obvious': The Renarrativizing of Postrevolutionary Mexico." In *Fragments of a Golden Age: The Politics of Culture in Mexico Since 1940,* edited by Gilbert M. Joseph et al., 234–272. Durham: Duke University Press, 2001.

INDEX

Printed in the United States
70412LV00001B/275

9 781403 966353